HORST PO

Paris • London •

HORST PORTRAITS

Paris • London • New York

Selected and with an essay by Terence Pepper
Notes on plates by Robin Muir

NATIONAL PORTRAIT GALLERY

Horst: Portraits
Paris, London, New York

Published in Great Britain by National Portrait Gallery Publications,
National Portrait Gallery, St Martin's Place, London WC2H 0HE

Published to accompany the exhibition *Horst Portraits: 60 Years of Style* held
at the National Portrait Gallery, London, from 1 March to 3 June 2001, and at the Museum of Fine Arts,
Boston, from 21 October 2001 to 6 January 2002.

For a complete catalogue of current publications, please write to the address above, or visit
our website at www.npg.org.uk/publications

ISBN hb 1 85514 292 9
ISBN pb 1 85514 325 9

A catalogue record for this book is available from the British Library.

Publishing Manager: Jacky Colliss Harvey
Senior Editor: Anjali Bulley
Production: Ruth Müller-Wirth
Design: Price Watkins
Photography: Michael Dyer Associates
Printed and bound in Italy by EBS, Verona

Front cover: Jessica Tandy, New York, 1938
Frontispiece: Rita Hayworth, New York, 1947

Sponsored in London by R E D W O O D

CONTENTS

Preface

6

Foreword Charles Saumarez Smith

7

Always in Vogue Terence Pepper

8

Plates

51

Notes on the plates Robin Muir

186

Acknowledgements

212

PREFACE

The possibility of staging a Horst exhibition at the National Portrait Gallery first occurred to me when I visited Hamiltons Gallery in Mayfair to see the first British exhibition of his work. Comprising 200 photographs, it coincided with Horst's eightieth birthday in August 1986.

Thinking of Horst up to that time as primarily a fashion photographer, I was surprised at the large number of portraits in the show that were accompanied by long informative captions written by Valentine Lawford. Lawford's book, *Horst: His Work and His World*, had been published in Britain the previous year. In consultation with my fellow curators, I suggested a number of photographs might be purchased for our collection, thus setting in train the possibility of a future show at the NPG. Regrettably, the three carefully selected photographs were declined by the then Trustees of the Gallery, but the subjects are, I am glad to say, now included in this exhibition.

In the intervening years, Horst's significance as an artist has grown immeasurably, and the attitude to collecting and exhibiting photographs has changed, particularly in this Gallery. In 1989 Horst generously donated a large-format platinum print of Noël Coward which formed one of the star items in the exhibition *Camera Portraits: Photographs from the National Portrait Gallery 1839-1989*. It was the National Portrait Gallery's first exhibition to travel to America and Japan and was curated by the Gallery's then Deputy Director, Malcolm Rogers. Dr Rogers has since become Director of the Museum of Fine Arts, Boston and we are delighted that he will be hosting this exhibition there.

In 1999 Hamiltons Gallery, in partnership with the German photographic collector and businessman Gert Elfering, purchased Horst's archive and house at Oyster Bay, Long Island, with the eventual aim of donating the archive to a new German state photography museum. Andrew Cowan and Tim Jefferies of Hamiltons generously offered us the first chance to view the archive and create the first Museum show of this collection. Horst had been in poor health and had previously moved to Florida. Sadly, the first of three Stateside visits I made in November 1999 to view and research in the archive coincided with the announcement of Horst's death. However, on my second visit, with the indefatigable help and enthusiasm of the Horst estate's archivist, Jennifer Gyr, and the calm good sense of my National Portrait Gallery colleague Beatrice Hosegood, the energetic spirit of Horst inspired us to continue and examine all surviving clues to his photographic sittings in the form of contact sheets, scrapbooks and rare vintage prints.

In selecting the exhibits, I have been very mindful of the current excellent publications of Horst's work, and I have attempted to find other unseen and interesting unpublished work. Out of necessity, already published iconic work has had to be included, but I trust that there is a sufficient difference and change of emphasis to make this collection an indispensable addition to Horst's very special vision of his world.

Terence Pepper
Curator of Photographs
National Portrait Gallery

FOREWORD

Shortly before Horst's death, Hamiltons Gallery in Mayfair acquired his photographic archive. We were approached as to whether or not we would like to mount a major retrospective exhibition of his portraits. We seized the opportunity with enthusiasm since Horst is so clearly one of the great, classic photographers of the twentieth century. Born in Germany, influenced by the work of the Bauhaus, trained at the Hamburg Kunstgewerbeschule and an assistant to Le Corbusier, his career epitomises the interconnections between art, fashion and high society in Paris, London and New York during the 1930s. In Paris, he was a friend of Jean Cocteau and Coco Chanel. In London, he photographed Cecil Beaton and Noël Coward. In New York, he used the same sense of dramatic composition and stylization to photograph the early stars of Hollywood. Although his work – so cool and so idealized – fell from fashion during the late 1950s, he remained an important influence on a younger generation, including Bruce Weber and Robert Mapplethorpe.

The quality of the exhibition is owing to the good eye and encyclopaedic knowledge of Terence Pepper, the Gallery's Curator of Photographs. I would also like to express our gratitude to Andrew Cowan and Tim Jefferies of Hamiltons Gallery who first suggested the exhibition and have supported it ever since. In addition, we are grateful to Redwood Publishing for their support of the exhibition in London.

Charles Saumarez Smith
Director
National Portrait Gallery

ALWAYS IN VOGUE

I like taking photographs, because I like life.
And I like photographing people best of all,
because most of all I love humanity[1].
Horst P. Horst

In the history of twentieth-century fashion and portrait photography, Horst's contribution figures as one of the most artistically significant and longest lasting, spanning as it did the sixty years between 1931 and 1991[2]. During this period, his name became legendary as a one-word photographic byline, and his photographs came to be seen as synonymous with the creation of images of elegance, style and rarefied glamour.

Born on 14 August 1906, Horst Paul Albert Bohrmann was the second son of a prosperous middle-class Protestant shop owner, Max Bohrmann, and his wife, Klara Schönbrodt. The four-storey family home was a sixteenth-century stone building in the Jüdenstraße in Weissenfels-an-der-Saale, a town in eastern Germany. On the ground floor was the Albert Bohrmann hardware shop, founded by Horst's grandfather and the source of the family's income.

Horst's mother had a love of history and a passion for nature, as well as being a compulsive collector of Meissen porcelain; she passed the first two qualities on to her son. Her family had their home thirty miles away at Bitterfeld in Saxony, and Horst's family visited there regularly. Three years younger than his brother Heinz, Horst spent much of his youth, feeling that he was being treated as second best, as his elder brother was being groomed to take over the family's fortunes and business and seemed to be his parents' favourite. This feeling determined Horst's later desire to move away and prove his individuality. His childhood years were nonetheless idyllic – he attended school in beautiful countryside – and the idyll ended only when his mother suffered a mental breakdown in 1913.

Max Bohrmann joined the army when war broke out in 1914. Although the family's financial situation deteriorated dramatically and food was hard to come by in the last year of the war, by the early 1920s their fortunes had recovered sufficiently for them to purchase a motor car and a second small holiday home. This was situated on a wooded hill called the Rosenberg outside Weimar, close to Max's sister Grete, whose house was constantly filled with young artists.

One of these, Eva Weidemann, ten years older than Horst, became his first intimate friend[3]. In a 1988 interview and photograph session, he chose to include a still-life photograph he had taken of a ceramic nude self-portrait that Eva had given him and that he still kept. A student of dance and drama at the Bauhaus, she introduced Horst to the world of art, poetry and theatre and to a group of friends who discussed the philosophies of Nietzsche and Kant and the paintings of Klee and Kandinsky. Their interests contrasted vividly with the stultifying life at Weissenfels. Eva took Horst to the opera and introduced him to the performances of Isadora Duncan and to Dalcroizian Eurythmics. The two friends discussed the intrinsic beauty of the human body and shared their interest in and acceptance of the cult of *Nacktkultur*, best experienced in the form of nude sunbathing.

To the more conservative inhabitants of Weimar, the Bauhaus group presented an unwelcome intrusion, and the group was forced to relocate to Dessau in 1925, much to the sorrow of Tante Grete. Just prior to this, Horst was sent to Leysin in Switzerland for treatment for a spot on his lung. During his year in the sanatorium there, he corresponded with Eva, who had gone to Capri following a falling-out with one branch of the Bauhaus theatre workshop. His plans to join her after his discharge from Leysin remained unfulfilled, however, and his disapproving parents forbade any further correspondence with her. Horst returned home to Weissenfels to think seriously about his future.

Encouraged by his father to do something academic, Horst went to Frankfurt to study Chinese with Richard Wilhelm, a translator of Lao-Tse, but the few months he spent there were not a success, and he moved on to a year's apprenticeship doing office work and filing letters in an import-export firm in Hamburg. (Horst's *Vogue* contemporary

Cecil Beaton endured a similar fate at his father's behest. Fortunately, both of these nascent artists escaped from their fathers' well-intentioned but impractical ideas.) Hamburg happened to be the home of the Kunstgewerbeschule, or School of Applied Art; Horst asked if he might work there when his year in import-export was complete. Remembering his interest in things artistic, his parents agreed, and he began what was to become a career in art and design by studying to be a carpenter and designing and making tables and chairs. This was a chance to be associated once again with the Bauhaus, as Walter Gropius and Marcel Breuer were then working on the modern furnishings for the SS *Bremen*. Horst's own furniture was modern and functional. Through another new friendship, he was encouraged to write to the Swiss-born French architect Le Corbusier, seeking work in his Paris atelier. Much to Horst's surprise, he received a favourable reply.

THE PARIS *BEAU MONDE*

Horst arrived in Paris in early 1930 and was quickly befriended by a number of useful contacts, including Robert de Saint-Jean and his friend Julien Green, the Paris-born American writer and novelist. Green later recalled how struck he was by Horst's intellectual curiosity and immense desire to learn. Before starting work with Le Corbusier, they visited churches and historical monuments, Versailles and the Louvre, thus providing Horst with a crash course in French history and culture. He was also much impressed by his first visit to an exhibition of Greek sculpture in a private gallery. These activities imbued Horst with ideas that he would use and adapt in his future career.

As an apprentice in Le Corbusier's studio, Horst was involved in a major commission to redesign a lavish apartment belonging to a Mexican millionaire, Don Carlos de Bestegui, on top of a building in the Champs Elysées. Photographs of the finished work were published in *Vogue* in 1932[4]. The most notable features were a golden modernist spiral staircase and a roof-garden whose shrubs could be rolled back to reveal views of Paris. Horst's task was to work on the design aspects of the bathroom, including the siting of two bidets to face each other. He quickly became disillusioned in the drab, grimy offices that housed the atelier and found himself unable to relate to Le Corbusier's rather frigid manner. When the studio closed for the summer, he had time to consider a change of direction.

Another chance encounter in a café led to an introduction to Gerald Kelly and his friend Baron George Hoyningen-Huene. The so-called 'Baltic Baron', whose father had been chief equerry to Tsar Nicholas II of Russia, had since 1926 been Chief Photographer for Paris *Vogue*, one of three editions of the magazine then in existence[5]. Huene worked in a style greatly influenced by *Vogue*'s star New York photographer, Edward Steichen. In Paris since the early 1920s, Huene had studied painting with the Cubist André Lhote, worked with Man Ray on a fashion portfolio and sold his own fashion drawings to *Harper's Bazaar* before taking up photography in 1925. Since then, his work had appeared in the French, British and American editions of *Vogue* and its allied publication *Vanity Fair*.

Horst and Huene were immediately attracted to one another, and Horst soon became Huene's photographic assistant, occasional model and travelling companion. Huene, although famous for his explosive temperament, was to remain a lifelong friend even though their close time together amounted to only a few years. On his death in 1968, he would leave all of his photographs to Horst, who combined them with his own to produce the memorial album *Salute to the Thirties* in 1971[6]. As Horst's mentor, Huene immediately introduced him to a wide group of artistic friends who dominated the social and artistic circles of Paris during one of its most important periods of cultural activity. This provided the perfect context for the beginning of Horst's self-taught career, the development of his aesthetic through his many visits to the Louvre, and his enjoyment of nineteenth-century English literature.

Horst and Huene's first trip abroad was to England in the winter of 1930. As well as visiting the Elgin Marbles at the British Museum, they travelled to Ashcombe, Cecil Beaton's country house in Wiltshire. There they were joined by the exotic fashion designer Charles James[7], the artist and stage and film designer Oliver Messel, Lord Jersey, Edith Oliver, Peter Watson, Lord and Lady Weymouth (later the Marquess of Bath and Mrs Daphne Fielding, respectively) and Beaton's two sisters Nancy and Baba. Beaton photographed Horst and Huene amongst the garden statuary, and Huene captured Beaton on film on his typically outlandish circus bed. Beaton was then the chief contributor to British *Vogue* and was making regular trips to New York and Paris, where he not only photographed but penned copy and created accompanying illustrations, caricatures and fashion drawings; an enviable work-load that few of his colleagues could match.

Horst at this time was not entirely at ease in the strange customs of English society and was not made entirely welcome by Beaton's occasional acid humour and disdainfulness. In later years with a career in common, Beaton eventually developed a grudging respect for Horst and each was to photograph the other with varying degrees of success over the following years.

Back in Paris in the spring of 1931, Huene took Horst to a lunch party to meet the American illustrator and artist Carl Erickson, known as 'Eric', and his wife Lee at their weekend apartment at Senlis. Also there was Dr Mehemed Agha, Art Director of American *Vogue*, who after a conversation about modern German photography enquired whether Horst would like to be a photographer himself. Horst surprised himself by saying 'yes', and Agha suggested that he should go twice a week to work at *Vogue*'s Paris studio.

With the help of Maurice, *Vogue*'s studio assistant, and building on the experience of observing and assisting Huene, Horst gradually picked up the rudiments of working with a 10-x-8 camera and taking exposures that could last between two and three seconds (this was before the era of light meters). The studio was well equipped, with a full complement of overhead lights and smaller spotlights whose arrangement would act as a trademark of Horst's evolving style. To begin with, this resembled a cross between the compositional approach of Steichen, *Vogue*'s leading photographer in New York, and Huene's restrained classicism.

The first pictures that carried a Horst credit line appeared in the December 1931 issue of French *Vogue*[8]. It was a full-page advertisement showing a model in black velvet holding a Klytia scent bottle in one hand with the other hand raised elegantly above it. There were also a number of small fashion and still-life photographs of artfully arranged accessories at the back of the magazine. Horst's real breakthrough as a published fashion and portrait photographer was in the pages of British *Vogue*. It was not until the June 1931 issue that Horst's first pictures of named subjects were published in French *Vogue*, and even then they only consisted of a selection of French society women glimpsed playing golf in the June 1932 issue, for which he shared the photographic credits with Huene.

Prior to this was a substantive body of work that appeared in British *Vogue* starting with the 30 March 1932 issue showing three fashion studies and a full-page portrait of the daughter of Sir James Dunn, the art patron and supporter of Surrealism. One of the fashion studies featured Norah Henderson, one of the cast of *Hold My Hand*, a musical comedy by Stanley Lupino that had opened the previous December at the Gaiety Theatre. This visit to London, unrecorded in Lawford's otherwise highly detailed biography, must have been made in December or early January in order to appear in the March issue. The star of the show and one of Britain's greatest musical stars of the 1930s was Jessie Matthews and Horst's picture of her garlanded in sequins and feathers was published in British *Vogue*'s 25 May 1932 issue prefiguring his sensational study of Mistinguett that appeared two years later.

Meanwhile, back in Paris, Horst was also taking portraits of celebrities and friends that were being sent for consideration to Dr Agha in New York for use in American *Vogue* or *Vanity Fair*. Though not published at the time, they include a number of significant subjects, including Rosa Covarrubias, wife of the celebrated Mexican artist Miguel Covarrubias, Francesco von Mendelssohn, cellist and Berlin producer of Noël Coward's early plays (plate 4), and Alan Pryce-Jones (plate 5), at the time a *Vogue* travel writer. These studies exhibit what was to become Horst's hallmark style of sensitive posing combined with sophisticated lighting arrangements. In the case of Covarrubias, they show a particular debt to Steichen in terms of pose[9].

Examples of these and other portraits have survived with Horst's technical and date annotations. Though experimental, they are highly proficient and were all eventually published. This is the body of work that helped to establish his early style. A number of pictures taken in his first months as a photographer appeared in an exhibition held in the basement of a bookshop called the Galerie La Plume d'Or in Passy at the start of 1932. One of these, taken at the end of 1931, is of Janet Flanner (fig.1), the influential Paris correspondent of the *New Yorker* since 1925, whose column, signed 'Genêt', reported back to America in one of that magazine's most-read regular features. Horst photographed Flanner, in profile, holding a monocle and a copy of the *New Yorker* in the guise of Eustace Tilly, the dandified figure who appeared on the first edition of the magazine and every subsequent anniversary cover. This and another portrait of Mrs Condé Nast were remarked on favourably by Flanner in a photographic review in the 27 February 1932 issue, in which she praised Horst's 'instinct for linear romance' learnt from the Bauhaus as an architecture and design student.

BERLIN, LONDON, NEW YORK

In March 1932, Horst accompanied Huene and Lucien Vogel, then art director of *Vu*, to Berlin, where the latter photographed Elisabeth Bergner and Brigitte Helm, the star of *Metropolis* who was then making *L'Atlantide* with G. W. Pabst. Helm's Classical Greek hair style, in this film about the lost city of Atlantis, would later be parodied by Huene in a spoof film in which his American painter friend Gerald Kelly played Helm's part. Horst was to recreate the same look in his portrait of the fashion model Helen Bennett in 1936 (plates 30 and 31).

After this Berlin adventure, Horst returned home briefly to Weissenfels, where his parents had become more reconciled to his choice of career. Then he had to rush to London to take his first significant portrait commission for American *Vogue* – Gertrude Lawrence – for publication in their July 1932 issue[10].

Lawrence, who had just returned from New York after appearing with Noël Coward in *Private Lives*, was not conventionally beautiful but knew how to pose naturally and elegantly in her Schiaparelli dress. Horst contributed his own specially designed background, lighting her from the side so she appears in mysterious half-shadow, and placing her on a zebra skin. Again, this portrait owes a debt in the formality of its composition to the highly regarded work of Steichen. Along with the favourable *New Yorker* review, it led Condé Nast, the founder, creator and Editor-in-Chief of *Vogue*, to invite Horst to work in New York on a six-month trial contract.

Horst arrived in New York on the *Ile-de-France* filled with expectations for his first trip to the New World, but his initial euphoria quickly turned to disappointment. The work he was given photographing American debutantes in an unfamiliar setting was infrequent

Fig.1 Janet Flanner as Eustace Tilly of the *New Yorker,* 1931

and unrewarding. Compared to the friendly staff at French *Vogue*, the New Yorkers he met were less helpful, placing outrageous demands on him that he was unable to satisfy. After about three months, he had a showdown with Condé Nast, who accused him of arrogance when he stated his hope to become as skilled as Steichen. This confrontation took place after a long discussion about every photograph Horst had taken to date; Nast had laid these out in his office and commented on how each might have been improved, with the Art Director present. Told to leave when his contract was up, Horst decided to return to Europe early, having effectively been sacked. In fact, some of the portraits he had taken were successful. His two studies of Hollywood stars

Fig.2 Condé Nast, New York, 1932

Adrienne Ames and the young Bette Davis both appeared as full pages in successive issues of *Vanity Fair*, while his studies of Kay Francis, who had recently returned to New York after three years, were spread over two pages of the September 1932 *Vogue*. One of the most significant pictures was a study of Condé Nast himself (fig.2). This definitive picture of him appeared on a full page in American *Vogue* in a tribute to the publisher at his death in 1942[11].

After his early return from America, Horst, at Huene's suggestion, took a break from photography for most of 1933. He spent his time in Tunisia supervising the building of their plaster and whitewash house overlooking the Bay of Hammamet. Re-energized by their break, Horst returned to Paris. French *Vogue* re-employed him, and new pictures of Lily Pons, the French-born American soprano, taken in the studio on 2 June 1933 appeared in French *Vogue*'s August issue (plate 21), while others of Florence Owen and Mme Arturo Ramos (neé Millicent Rogers) appeared in the November issue. On 21 December, Horst had an important session with the legendary French music hall star Mistinguett (plate 2). He pictured her in a symphony of different textures of white and cream, one arm jauntily poised at her waist and the other holding a bunch of large lilies, their tops suggestively touching her smiling mouth. Clothed in a typical Molyneux white silk sheath gown with an ostrich-feather hat and trimmings, she posed against a suitably feathered and dramatically lit *mise-en-scène*. The portrait publicized the star's new revue, *Folies en Folies*, at the Folies-Bergère. This is the earliest in what was to become the series of Horst's classic portraits that were reprinted as platinum prints in the 1980s. Other photographs from the sitting show Mistinguett seated in front of two veined marble columns, without her ostrich hat, showing off her famous and characteristic coiffure to full advantage (plate 3).

Horst's study of the American-born decorator and interior designer Elsie de Wolfe, Lady Mendl, posed in front of Boldini's 1905 portrait of her (plate 6), was also first published in 1933 and is linked to two similar studies taken by Huene of the Vicomtesse de Noailles in front of her Bérard portrait and of the Princess Jean-Louis de Faucigny-Lucigne in front of hers by Laglenne. These pictures emphasize the close links in composition and interpretation between the two allied media, as well as the two photographers' approach to portraiture[12]. Huene's work is marked by a cool, uncluttered classicism with which Horst also flirted at times. More frequently, Horst eschewed this approach for aspects of baroque romanticism in his choice of constructed settings, elaborate props and sculptural compositions achieved with low-level lighting and carefully placed spots, focused on limited areas of generally dark compositions[13].

In the following year, Huene was sent to the West Coast of America to photograph a number of Hollywood stars, including Carol Lombard, Dolores del Rio and Katharine Hepburn, for *Vanity Fair* and French *Vogue*. In his absence, Horst was given many of the more important commissions that Huene, as Chief Photographer, might otherwise have fulfilled. Before setting off, Huene lent Horst his apartment and commissioned Bérard to paint Horst's portrait. A highly esteemed artist and stage designer, Christian 'Bébé' Bérard had been talent-spotted for *Vogue* by the Editor Michel de Brunhoff, who used his graphic skills for fashion illustration and cover art. Horst had first met Bérard in Monte Carlo in the winter of 1931, when he had travelled there to assist Huene in taking pictures of Colonel de Basil's new Ballets Russes production of *Cotillon*, for which Bérard was designing the sets and costumes. Horst photographed Bérard on a number of occasions in his short life, here he is seen mixing paints while decorating a screen in the Paris apartment of Captain Edward Molyneux, the British-born couturier (plate 7).

A MODISH YOUNG MAN

In 1934 Horst made several appearances in British *Vogue*, beginning with his series of portraits for Noël Coward's new production *Conversation Piece*, a play with music set in the Regency period and featuring the French star Yvonne Printemps and the Mexican-born American actor, director and dramatist Romney Brent. Horst had first been impressed by English style, personified for him by the handsome Prince of Wales, while still in Germany; this style now reached its apogee, as he saw it, in Noël Coward. Horst admired Coward's urbanity and 'lightness of touch which was a mixture of show-off and throwaway that was endearing – a theatrical style, befitting his public image', as he later described Coward in an interview with Valentine Lawford[14]. The consummate photographs of Coward posing in a chair (plate 15) and in a group with Printemps and Brent (plate 14) were most likely both taken at the end of the year, when Coward was in Paris attending a British Embassy ball at which he and Printemps performed a cabaret[15]. Later Horst photographed Printemps and Coward in London in their Regency costumes during rehearsals for the production, which opened on 16 February 1934 at His Majesty's Theatre; these pictures were also used in America in *Vanity Fair* when the production was restaged on Broadway. The play was a popular rather than a critical success and is now remembered for featuring Coward's autobiographical hit song *I'll Follow My Secret Heart*. In 1936 Horst would work with Coward again, this time for the production of *Tonight at 8.30*, a series of three one-act plays, produced on both sides of the Atlantic.

'The London Collections Seen with a Parisian Eye' was the banner headline announcing the lead item in British *Vogue*, 4 April 1934. This headline emphasized Horst's growing importance as a photographer, he had been invited to London to photograph and comment in a long article recording his reactions to the various fashion houses. *Vogue*'s copywriter continued: 'A modish young man comes over from Paris and looks at the London Fashion collections with a fresh and unbiased eye. Some of the loveliest models from the English dress houses are photographed here by Horst in illustration of his view.' As well as photographing Douglas Fairbanks Jnr, Horst shot a number of London socialites, including Lady Jersey, the Australian-born second wife of the 9th Earl, Viscountess Ridley, daughter of the architect Edwin Lutyens, Mrs Anthony Eden, wife of the then Lord Privy Seal, and a quartet of debutantes[16]. As photographic portraits, his two studies of the fabulously dressed 19-year-old Princess Karam of Kapurthala are the most impressive. In one study, she wears traditional silken saris, while in the other she is posed in Paquin's black evening coat trimmed with silver fox (plate 19).

When not on *Vogue* assignments, Horst had time to renew his acquaintance with Oliver Messel, Beaton's rival as a stage designer, and Peter Watson, at the time the love of Beaton's life. Messel and Watson took Horst to lunch with two of the Mitford sisters, Diana and Unity, whose romantic liaisons with Oswald Mosley and Adolf Hitler had necessarily tragic outcomes. Nada Ruffer, then Fashion Editor on *Vogue*, took him to a charity ball with an outrageously daring night-club act performed by Messel, Sarah Churchill and David Herbert.

In the absence of a *Vogue* studio in London, Horst used the studio of the leading portrait photographer Howard Coster, located off the Strand (Huene also worked here on his London visits). Coster's own portrait styles relied on low lighting and dramatic use of spots and had much in common with Horst, as is particularly apparent in some of his fashion work for *Vogue*. Coster's photograph of Horst announced a special portfolio of work taken for British *Vogue* in October 1934. Horst's other significant London fashion sessions were done on later visits with Vivien Leigh and Merle Oberon. Both stars were at early stages in their careers and agreed to frequent requests from *Vogue* to model clothes. Oberon's dark features are dramatically shown off in one of

Horst's cave-type sets which he spent days constructing (plate 20) and is typical of his period of baroque romanticism.

Back in Paris for his socially most important sitting to date, Horst was invited to take exclusive pictures of the 28-year-old Princess Marina of Greece shortly before her wedding in London to the third son of King George V and Queen Mary, Prince George, Duke of Kent. Marina and her sister had been at finishing school in Paris and were based there in the months leading up to the wedding. This marriage into the British Royal Family also elevated Marina's budding status as a fashion leader.

Horst went to considerable trouble in designing a setting and finding props for a series of photographs of Marina that were published on several occasions[17]. In the best-known one, she wears a grey silk evening dress by Molyneux (plate 18). Posing her at the left, with one hand resting casually against a large column and standing at a slight angle on a rich Savonnerie carpet with a luxuriant floral pattern, Horst photographed the Princess with her eyes slightly averted as if in reverie. The inclusion of a dark grey velvet curtain behind her helps to emphasize the drapes and folds of the silver-grey dress. The curtain is partly drawn aside from the right-hand side of the composition to reveal a false architectural background made from a huge photographic blow-up of a reproduction of Veronese's *Cena in casa di Levi*, 1573, of the interior of a palazzo to which an ornate piece of furniture was added to introduce a sense of depth. A small framed print of this photograph was one of only three photographs that Horst always kept on display at his home in Oyster Bay, Long Island, thus emphasizing his pleasure at having taken it and its importance to his career[18]. This mildly baroque, evenly lit *tour de force* contrasts with another study of the Hellenic Princess posed simply in front of a marble relief, which uses spotlights to emphasize the modelling of her head and shoulders (draped in white) and thus encapsulates the two differing styles in which Horst could work.

Also while Huene was away, Horst contributed a large number of pages to British and French *Vogue* covering the various collections and took the first of a number of subjects dressed for elaborate costume balls. Horst had attended the earliest of these balls, arranged by Baron Nicolas 'Niki' de Gunzburg and co-hosted by Prince and

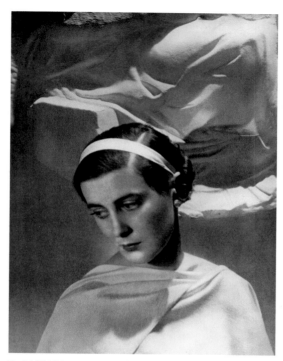

Fig.3 HRH Princess Marina of Greece, Paris, 1934

Princess Jean-Louis de Faucigny-Lucigne, in June 1934. Entitled 'A Night at Schönbrun' in some accounts and 'Le Bal de Valses' in others, it was held in the Bois de Bologne on an island, and the guests came dressed as members of the Hapsburg Court of the 1860s. Sparing no expense, costumes were designed by Bérard, Alix, Mainbocher and Lanvin and made by Mme Karinska of the Ballets Russes. Horst, as well as appearing as a hussar, was asked to photograph the hosts and principal guests at the *Vogue* studio on the evening prior to the event. Twelve of these romantic portraits, resembling a cross between daguerreotypes and Winterhalter portraits, were published over a two-page spread, all of them fairly small, in the August 1934 issue; they included de Gunzburg as Archduke Rudolph, Princess Jean-Louis de Faucigny-Lucigne as the tragic Empress Elizabeth, Don Carlos de Bestegui and Lady Mendl. In a group photograph taken on the night, Horst found himself next to Coco Chanel, whose path would cross his many times. In fact, a deep friendship grew between them after Horst took in 1937 what became – to her and most others – her definitive portrait photograph (plate 32).

Huene eventually returned from America to find that his relations with *Vogue* were becoming strained. Frank Crowninshield, the Editor of *Vanity Fair*, complained about the lack of close-ups in Huene's Hollywood portraits[19]. When Huene met Dr Agha to renegotiate his contract, he was reprimanded and resigned in a fury. He then contacted Carmel Snow, Editor of rival *Harper's Bazaar*, offering his services. Huene disliked the portrait of Horst that he had commissioned from Bérard, and so it passed to Horst himself, who was also given the use of Huene's apartment. In future Huene would stay as often as possible at their house at Hammamet and visit Paris only to carry out commissions from his new employer.

Huene's permanent absence from *Vogue* provided Horst with his second chance of working for the American edition, perhaps made possible through the intercession of Iva Patcevitch, who had worked with Crowninshield on *Vanity Fair*. It was agreed that Horst, although based in America, would make two or three trips a year to Paris and London to cover the collections and other important sittings.

Staying in New York at the Gladstone Hotel on East 52nd Street between Park and Lexington Avenues, Horst found himself among European émigré friends such as Pavel Tchelitchew and Eleonora and Francesco von Mendelssohn. With a new salary of $20,000 a year, he was well able to afford the good life, and his working relationship with Condé Nast, Edna Chase, Dr Agha and even Margaret Chase, the Society Editor, improved enormously now that he was older and more experienced.

In the summer of 1935, before returning to Europe, he visited the West Coast for the first time to see Hollywood, where several friends including Natasha Paley, Niki de

Gunzburg, Erik Charell and Oliver Messel were at work. Paley was appearing in a small part in *Sylvia Scarlett*, and Messel was designing sets and costumes for *Romeo and Juliet*. Horst only took a few snapshots, which included George Cukor and Katharine Hepburn (plate 27), the director and star of *Sylvia Scarlett* respectively, as well as Messel (plate 26) and the English child star Freddie Bartholomew. These were Horst's first photographs taken with a Rolleiflex, a camera that Condé Nast disallowed in the *Vogue* studio, believing that the technical perfection required for his magazine could only be properly achieved on 10-x-8 inch negatives. In her photograph, Hepburn has her hair short, as her character *Sylvia Scarlett* required her to be disguised as a boy to escape from France. Interestingly the film was later condemned by the Legion of Decency for its alleged coded homosexuality.

Back in Paris, the rage for costume balls was in full flow. Such events took on great importance as reflections of the hedonistic lifestyle enjoyed by the top figures in French society. This lifestyle was echoed in London, where Mme Yevonde made lavish costume pictures based on a 'Gods and Goddesses' party held at the Ritz[20]. Marie-Laure, Vicomtesse de Noailles was perhaps one of the most outstanding figures of 1930s Parisian society, both as a painter and author of three novels and, with her husband, as a patron of avant-garde and controversial modern art. They sponsored Buñuel's surrealist film *L'Age d'Or* (1930) and Cocteau's *Le Sang d'un Poète* (1931). Their art collection included cutting-edge artists Dalí, Bérard and de Chirico. Horst photographed the Vicomtesse (fig.4) as a Florentine youth from the days of the Medici in an outfit designed by Schiaparelli set off by a Suzy pill-box hat that was accorded a full-page reproduction in the various editions of July 1935 *Vogue*. The inspiration for this image was a major Franco-Italian festival that included an exhibition of Renaissance masterpieces at the Petit Palais and Jeu de Paume. (The festival had a direct impact on the fashion houses and was reflected in the outfit worn by Princess Scherbatov in Horst's first cover photograph for *Vogue* in September 1935.

For the July 1935 feature, Horst photographed the statuesque Russian-born Iya, Lady Abdy, who wrote and played in *Les Cenci*. This entertainment also formed part of the Franco-Italian festivities and had costumes designed by Balthus and made by Mme

Fig.4 Marie-Laure, Vicomtesse de Noailles, Paris, 1935

Karinska and Agnes. Born Marguerite but known as 'Daisy', the Hon. Mrs Reginald Fellowes (plate 11) was another important Paris socialite of taste, intelligence and influence. That same summer, she staged Le Bal Oriental; Horst showed her with exotically arranged hair sculpted by Antoine and a gown by Schiaparelli. Other well-known Horst photographs from this ball include that of Misia Sert (plate 10), the Russian-born second wife of the Spanish painter José Maria Sert, masked, dressed in black silk pyjamas and wearing a tall conical hat and feather plume, and Elsa

Fig.5 Elsa Schiaparelli as a Venetian blackamoor, Paris, 1935

Schiaparelli as a blackamoor (fig.5). Martinez de Hoz is pictured as Watteau's *Gilles* in the white silk costume she wore for the 'Masterpieces of Paintings' ball sponsored by Count Etienne de Beaumont (plate 12). Though not strictly part of this series, Horst's striking advertisement enacted the following year for the luxury department store Bergdorf Goodman of the dancer Tamara Geva with a young Arab attendant would appear to draw its inspiration from these fantastic and lavishly staged events (plate 13).

THE RISE OF THE FASHION MODEL

Condé Nast, as well as being responsible for the promotion of great photography in his magazines, was equally keen to innovate and introduce colour photography as soon as the relevant technical and printing problems could be solved. Having acquired the *Vogue* title in 1906, he gradually introduced more photographs into the magazine but continued to commission fashion illustrations until his reader surveys convinced him that the public would prefer photographs. In 1932 Steichen contributed the first photographic cover to *Vogue*, and throughout the 1930s there continued an even mix between photography and drawn and graphic art. Horst had his chance to produce his first colour cover – showing Adelaide Munroe, Princess Scherbatov (the daughter of an American diplomat married to a Russian prince) – in September 1935. Posed at an angle over a prop balustrade, she is pictured half-length in a strong graphic composition. The photograph, which shows off her Italian-inspired Veronese-red velveteen jacket, appeared on all three *Vogue* editions. This was the first of more than eighty covers that Horst was selected to shoot over the next twenty years.

Horst's best cover work was done with models with whom he built up a strong rapport such as Lisa Fonssagrives, whom he often described as his favourite model; others from the 1930s included Helen Bennett, Muriel Maxwell and Lud. Horst may justly be credited with the promotion of the fashion model and the discovery of some of those individuals who had especially rewarding careers. Previously in *Vogue*, society women had been persuaded to model clothes, but they lacked the skills and capabilities that a dedicated photographer's model can bring to a partnership.

Although his first cover with Fonssagrives did not happen until 1940, after she had moved to New York, Horst was one of the earliest photographers to work with her and spot her potential (plates 64, 73 and 91)[21]. Fonssagrives had been introduced to him in Paris in 1936 through another photographer, Willy Maywald, and Mme Dile, manager of the French *Vogue* studio. Fonssagrives, like Horst before her, went to the Louvre to observe how models posed in paintings and see what she could learn from this for her photographic sittings. Helen Bennett (plates 30 and 31) was an American model and one of the first that Horst brought over to Paris from New York to photograph for the collections and fashion pictures. Standing on a pedestal holding up her cape, she is an archetypal Horst construction, combining his love of Greek art and his distancing of his subjects onto a raised plane, literally on this occasion. Horst discovered Lud when she delivered a package to *Vogue* and he asked her to model for him. Single-minded and with an aversion to jewellery, she nevertheless revolutionized modelling with her sensual, catlike characteristics. In his most classical composition, she models a Grecian column-shaped dress by Alix, posed between two huge cylindrical columns made from paper rolls (plate 46). Lud later married a lion tamer and went off on tour with his circus before returning to act as a house model for Schiaparelli after World War II. Horst's other regular models in the 1930s included Lyla Zelensky and Blanche Grady, while in the 1940s and 1950s he created significant pictures with Bettina Bollegard, Betty McLaughlin, Carmen and Suzy Parker, and, a decade later, with Veruschka.

THE NEW CELEBRITIES

Back in New York as the 1930s drew to a close, Horst noted that a new sort of subject was taking over photographers' attention. 'Hollywood movie stars', he wrote in the introduction to his memoir *Salute to the Thirties*, ' – whether American or European born – imperceptibly assumed the place left vacant by Europe's vanished or vanishing Royalties.' It was evident that with the approach of war and the accompanying uncertainty, readers of *Vogue* and other periodicals felt an insatiable desire to subscribe to the escapism offered by the films and lives of the new Hollywood stars. Horst now began to photograph these classless subjects, whose fame sprang from their thespian skills rather than from inherited wealth or social position.

Olivia de Havilland (plate 34), having recently completed *Call it a Day*, was framed by Horst in a real Old Master frame in a variation of the *trompe l'œil* motif he also used in his Schiaparelli portrait (plate 22). He went to surrealist extremes in 1935 in Magritte-like photographs of Lady Pamela Smith gazing into a mirror in which a different image of her appears and photographed Frances Farmer in 1939 holding a miniature of the same photograph that Horst had made of her[22]. His study of Olive Deering and Eleonora von Mendelssohn (fig.6) transposes his *trompe l'œil* approach to a stage setting showing them through a torn paper frame among a stylized Greek setting for Robert Turney's play *Daughters of Arteus* (1936). He photographed Bette Davis (plate 40) like Tom Thumb in a huge prop chair seen on the Warner Brothers lot

Fig.6 Eleonora von Mendelssohn and Olive Deering in *Daughters of Arteus*, New York, 1936

in Hollywood; but this time in a Nettie Rosenstein dress, with a new-look 1940s hair style, for a *Vogue* sitting. In contrast to these special effects, Deanna Durbin (plate 35), the child star, was photographed in a light and wholesome manner in contrast to the brooding, powerful iconography of Joan Crawford (plate 41), whose large hat, heavily made-up face and bow-shaped mouth make her stand out against another of Horst's enlarged Old Master backgrounds[23].

The New York theatre also provided Horst with new subjects, such as Emlyn Williams (plate 43) in the thriller *Night Must Fall*. This portrait conveys menace through its use of a darkened silhouette in which Williams's spiky gesture suggests unease. Hand gestures also play an important part in the study of Ethel Waters (plate 42) as Hagar in *Mamba's Daughters*, but in this case it is to intensify an atmosphere of pain and struggle. In contrast, Horst's more brightly lit portraits of Tallulah Bankhead (plate 72) and Jessica Tandy (plate 47) show more of his dexterity. Bankhead, whom he was also to photograph in productions of Thornton Wilder's *Skin of Their Teeth* and Cocteau's *The Eagle Has Two Heads*, is shown here as Regina Giddens in Lillian Hellman's *The Little Foxes. Vogue* presciently dubbed this one of her most important roles in a feature celebrating Bankhead and Laurette Taylor. Jessica Tandy, the English-born actress who married Jack Hawkins and then Hume Cronyn and settled in America, was the first person to play Blanche du Bois on Broadway in *A Streetcar Named Desire*. Horst set her against a curved modernist block suggesting Bauhaus-inspired furnishings to create one of his most classically composed and aesthetically perfect pictures which also manages to be remote and dream-like, drawing on an actor's ability to entrance.

THE GATHERING STORM

The onset of World War II saw the closure of French *Vogue* in 1940 after a raid by the Occupation forces. Michel de Brunhoff was to lose his son when he was caught working for the Resistance shortly before the end of the war, and the magazine was not back in production until the special Liberation issue of February 1945. In America, the first few years of the war did not appear to have much effect on the contents of *Vogue*. With the closure of fashion houses in Paris, fashion was now American led. Meanwhile, Condé Nast urged all of the *Vogue* photographers to produce more naturalistic outdoor photographs, which new staff such as Toni Frissell had been contributing regularly since the mid-1930s. This action photography, also pioneered by Norman Parkinson, contrasted strongly with Horst's and Beaton's studio-based work.

War was declared between America and Germany on 7 December 1941. Horst was called up for service, though he was not officially enrolled until July 1943. The late 1930s and early 1940s were his most productive years, during which he excelled at working with 10-x-8 inch colour transparencies both for covers and for portrait and fashion sittings. Arturo Toscanini (plate 60) was in New York with eleven members of his family, who were all present while Horst attempted to take the first colour photograph of the 'greatest conductor of his time'[24]. A sitting with the dancer Alicia

Markova was for a feature in which she was one of several subjects photographed to show how 'famous hands have moulded careers'. This alternative illustration (plate 61) is a more compléte portrait. The portrait of Lily Cushing (plate 70), seen at work on one of her paintings, which includes a classical sculpted torso in the left-hand corner, is regrettably Horst's only colour photograph of an artist in their atelier.

Horst's European acquaintances who had gone to New York to escape hostilities included fashion designer Valentina (plate 23) and Lady Mendl. Horst later photographed them in colour as well as actresses including the British-born Leonora Corbett and the French film star Annabella. American film stars captured in colour included Paulette Goddard (plate 66), wife of Charlie Chaplin, who was shown modelling an exotic Hattie Carnegie two-piece Hawaiian beach outfit. Gene Tierney, the star of *The Male Animal*, appeared on the cover of *Vogue* in a 'peppermint striped playsuit with paradoxical long sleeves' while surrounded by decorative umbrellas[25]. In a Surrealist-inspired study, she features in another issue flanked by masks made by Lillian Bettinger, and captioned improvingly with four lines of poetry by W. B. Yeats ending, 'I'm looking for the face I had before the world was made' (plate 62).

As a typical example of wartime escapism, the Rita Hayworth film *Cover Girl* (1944) provided Horst with the opportunity to produce one of his most sumptuous film-star covers in a montage of seven different portraits of the cover girl Susann Shaw set against a silk design. His picture of Loretta Young became an almost immediate classic when it was featured in a special edition of *Vogue* which included masterpieces of photography selected by Steichen to show off the first hundred years of the medium. Earlier in 1938, Horst had photographed Young in a 'symphony of tulle': this time she was set off in a black silk crêpe dress and huge Lilly Dache picture hat of 'yellow spun glass and black lace'. Her red nail varnish finds colour matches in her carnation and lipsticked mouth in this carefully choreographed composition (plate 67).

Condé Nast's special photography issue also included a survey requesting readers to write in to say which of two photographs of the same models and garments taken by two photographers they preferred. One was a studio set-up, the other an outdoor 'natural' setting; the first was by Horst, the second by Toni Frissell, the society

Fig. 7 Lady Diana and Alfred Duff Cooper, New York, 1940

girl-turned-action photographer. Condé Nast believed that the public would vote overwhelmingly for the second picture, but in fact the opposite happened. However, he ignored the results, and the outdoor picture became the new norm. In the post-war period, this perceived naturalness and the 'all-American look' were to become the styles that editors such as Jessica Daves would promote. This was not what Horst was best at or enjoyed, and although he was to work for *Vogue* for the next four decades, it was not until the 1980s that his pre-war style became fashionable again and he could recreate the style he had pioneered in the 1930s.

Other subjects in New York in the early 1940s included two much-admired Chinese women – the writer Helena Kuo (plate 28) and Mrs Wellington Koo, wife of the diplomat and former ambassador to London – as well as a number of visiting Britons anxious to bring attention to the situation in Europe before America joined the conflict. Two of the most important sittings from the social editors' point of view were a group photograph of Alfred Duff Cooper (later Viscount Norwich) and his wife, the society beauty Lady Diana Cooper, who were in New York at the start of a lecture tour (fig.7) – Horst made this one of his best double portraits as well as taking Lady Diana Cooper alone (plate 77) – and Lady Mountbatten, wife of Lord Louis Mountbatten, Admiral of the Fleet and future Viceroy of India. Lady Mountbatten was visiting in her official capacity as a representative of the British Red Cross and president of the St John's Ambulance Brigade. Under the patronage of Queen Mary, her task was to engineer the sale of British lace in America and Canada for the war effort. This is Horst's only photograph of a woman in uniform (fig.8). Caught up in other ways in the relief effort for Britain was Merle Oberon, the star of *Wuthering Heights*, who had become Lady Korda since Horst had last photographed her (plate 52). Oberon was on her way to Hollywood and had just been on a five-week tour of American Expeditionary Force camps in England and Ireland acting as Mistress of Ceremonies for a USO entertainment troupe. For *Vogue*, she was involved in the 'Bundles for Britain' appeal, which was being vigorously publicized to help make up for shortages back in Europe.

Other classic photographs taken in 1942 include Horst's two studies of Marlene Dietrich, a fellow German to whom he could speak in his native language and for whom he created one of her defining images. Ignoring her advice to follow her director Josef von Sternberg's preferred method of lighting her, Horst brought the spotlight down below her face, which both softened the picture and eliminated any wrinkles (plates 54 and 55). This soft, dark light also pervades his study of the two leads of the play *Liliom*, Burgess Meredith and Ingrid Bergman (plate 50).

Also in New York in the 1940s was Wallis Simpson, Duchess of Windsor, who was spending part of the war there with the exiled Duke of Windsor, Governor of the Bahamas. He had photographed her shortly after her marriage in France in 1937, during an exclusive *Vogue* sitting in her suite at the Hotel Meurice in Paris (plate 33).

Fig. 8 Lady Louis Mountbatten, New York, 1940

This session was documented in the magazine by three photographs of Horst at work taken by Roger Schall. Horst photographed the Duchess lying on a chaise longue as her dress was too tight and she was uncomfortable standing. Horst's third sitting with the Duchess occurred in 1943 at her New York home in the Waldorf Tower, part of the Waldorf Astoria Hotel[26]. He positioned her emerging from the bedroom and standing in the light-coloured doorway, which set off her very slim silhouette (plate 58). The Duchess appears pencil-thin and elegant, shown at an angle with her arms posed carefully, one at her hip and the other holding the door handle. To the right, the framed print and rounded chair and cushion balance the composition. The close-fitting plain crêpe dress decorated with small bows is yet another design by Mainbocher, by then resident in New York.

A colour portrait of Mrs Wellington Koo was one of Horst's last pictures to be published in American *Vogue* before his enlistment in the Army and his eventual stationing at Fort Belvoir, Virginia. His recruitment also confirmed his status as an American citizen. It was then that he officially abandoned his surname of Bohrmann and adopted Horst P. Horst as his American name, although he remained Horst for future photographic purposes. He became an official Army Photographer with work published in the local forces' magazine. A survey of his portraits was published at the end of 1944 as *Photographs of a Decade*.

Three weeks before the war ended in 1945, President Franklin D. Roosevelt died and Harry S. Truman became President. Horst, still in the Army, was commissioned to take some official photographs a fortnight after Truman's inauguration. This sitting was to be the start of a number of commissions associated with the White House, including portraits of the First Ladies up to the Nixon and Ford years. Truman's picture appeared in *Vogue* with the credit: 'U.S. Signal Corps Photographer – Horst'.

POST-WAR TRAVELS
Once discharged, Horst returned to commercial photography with a new contract for *Vogue* offered by Alexander Liberman, who had succeeded Dr Agha as Art Director. Liberman had been responsible for helping to realize Horst's *Vogue* cover of a model lying upside down balancing a huge ball to form the letter 'O' in *Vogue*[27]. Liberman in the meantime had recruited a new team of photographers, the most influential of whom was Irving Penn. In a classic group photograph taken in the style of a Courbet conversation piece, Penn recorded most of the new *Vogue* status quo (in a picture that showed (from left to right): Serge Balkin, Cecil Beaton, George Platt Lynes, Kostia Joffe, the model Dorian Leigh, Horst, Penn himself and Erwin Blumenfeld. *Vogue* also had new larger, well-equipped studios, and photographers were permitted to use the less cumbersome Rolleiflex camera, which took $2\frac{1}{4}$ inch negatives.

Towards the end of 1945, Horst had travelled to Mexico with Huene in order to take a wide-ranging series of photographs of prominent figures including Carlos Chavez (plate 87), the distinguished composer, as well as film-makers, literary figures and Cantinflas, the comic, later known internationally for his role in *Around the World in Eighty Days*. The resulting six-page feature also included photographs of four artists, among them David Alfaro Siqueiros holding a huge self-portrait and Mexico's most renowned artist, Diego Rivera, sitting in Ciro's restaurant below a large mural of a nude[28]. Feeling that this photograph by itself lacked sufficient interest, Horst made it into one of his *trompe l'œil* montages by adding pages from his scrapbooks and reproductions of Rivera's paintings of Dolores del Rio and Frida Kahlo (plate 88).

The Mexico pictures appeared in the same issue of American *Vogue* that recorded the early results of Horst's first post-war visit to Paris in 1946. He compiled a photographic report to run alongside Eric's (Carl Erickson) illustrations to show the first new Paris collections. Further coverage was devoted to contemporary political and artistic personalities, including two former Prime Ministers, Léon Blum and Eduard Herriot, the painters André Marchand and Leonor Fini (plate 57), and the composer and organist Olivier Messiaen surrounded by a group of interested students (plate 81). Best known from this particular assignment are Horst's studies of Gertrude Stein. Horst was introduced to Stein by the fashion designer Balmain, who had provided a refuge for her and her companion, Alice B. Toklas, at his home in the Alps during the war. After photographing her with a model at Balmain's showroom, Horst was permitted to visit and photograph her at her apartment with her poodle, Basket, and the dog's portrait by Marie Laurençin (plate 82). This was the last frame that Horst took during this session, but others – such as his self-portrait standing behind Stein while she is being drawn by Eric – have become equally iconic (fig.9). The finished drawing by Eric appeared in British and French *Vogue*, instead of Horst's now classic photograph. On the same visit to Paris, Horst met up with old friends such as Chanel and Louise de Vilmorin and took more photographs of Janet Flanner.

Back in New York, Horst had his first sittings with Carmen Dell'Orefice. Newly discovered by *Vogue*, Carmen had trained as a ballet dancer and was a champion swimmer. She has maintained her status as a top model and New York personality up to the present day, acting as muse to many of the world's greatest fashion photographers. Her first

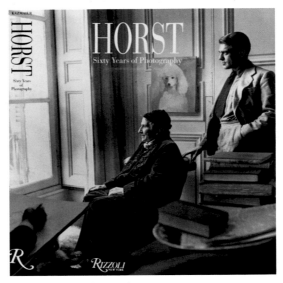

Fig. 9 Self-portrait with Gertrude Stein, Paris, 1946
(Jacket cover for *Horst: Sixty Years of Photography*, Schirmer/Mosel
Verlag, 1991; Rizzoli International Publications, 1991)

published pictures were taken by Clifford Coffin and appeared in the February 1946 issue of American *Vogue*; these were quickly followed by now classic photographs by Blumenfeld and Beaton. Richard Avedon's photographs of her, taken in Paris in 1957, formed an important part of his 1982 show at the Metropolitan Museum of Art, New York. Carmen's collaboration with Norman Parkinson began in the late 1940s and continued into the 1950s and 1960s, and Parkinson was instrumental in relaunching her career as a million-dollar model at the age of sixty[29].

Carmen's second photographic session for *Vogue* was with Horst in June 1946, having appeared in an American *Vogue* spread by Coffin. It shows the 15-year-old surrounded by a white gown in preparation for a facial massage, accentuating her remarkable eyes and face. Horst's test shot of Carmen in a Renaissance portrait style conveys well her fragile yet determined beauty (plate 76). In the following year, *Vogue* asked its top four photographers – Erwin Blumenfeld, Irving Penn, John Rawlings and Horst – to select their favourite subject for a new portrait. Horst chose Carmen and constructed a romantic, surreal study with a revealing and deeply felt accompanying text:

> Little Carmen is the ideal painter's beauty ... she possesses an
> inherent gracefulness rarely found except in primitive races.
> Her almond-shaped eyes are those of a Renaissance beauty, a soft
> revelation when looking up – she tends to keep her well-defined
> eye-lids cast down over them. The planes of her face are those of
> a Botticelli page, her long neck that of figure of Spring ... She
> has two primary requisites of true elegance: the physical attributes
> of youth and the languor of the past. She is an American beauty
> of an antique other age.

Horst's lyrical description set the scene for a number of further sittings, and Carmen paid one of the more touching tributes to him at his memorial service.

Horst continued to cover the Paris collections until 1951, working with Lisa Fonssagrives (plate 91), who had married Irving Penn in London in 1950. This was one of the great photographer-and-muse partnerships in the history of fashion photography. But the post-war fashion world was changing rapidly, and Horst found himself increasingly working on location. An assignment in Venice, photographing prominent Venetians and their families at their villas, was a precursor of the location work he was to do over the next twenty years[30]. This assignment included photographing his longstanding friend Jean Cocteau in St Marks Square (plate 83), as well as Cocteau's long-term companion, actor and artist Jean Marais (plate 85). Horst's study of Misia Sert with her little dog outside the Café Florian, with the canal and typical Venetian vista behind (plate 84), was his tribute to one of the most influential people in Paris at the turn of the century and throughout the 1920s. Horst's photograph, of a woman who had been painted by Toulouse-Lautrec and Bonnard, is a perfect summation of the Venice Sert knew and loved to walk around.

Horst's few important studio photographs from 1948 include a striking series of Edith Sitwell in colour and black-and-white showing off her remarkable jewellery. Horst provided the large prop book to suggest a link with literature and old England as well as creating a strong compositional contrast to her striking features (plate 69). Even more extreme, compositionally, is the group portrait he constructed in the studio of four New York beauties, dressed as 'Gibson Girls' (fig.10) for a special fund-raising ball that was to be held at the Plaza Hotel, and which appeared in American *Vogue*, December 1941. One beauty holds a hatpin, as she is about to skewer the luckless miniature man on the table, thus adding a bizarre touch to Charles Dana Gibson's launch of the 'Gibson Girls' in his book of collected drawings of Edwardian New Women entitled *The Weaker Sex*[31].

Following the closure of the studio at *Vogue* and honouring his wish to build his own house, Horst purchased land on the Tiffany estate at Oyster Bay on Long Island from the sale of a Picasso drawing that replaced a loan of many years earlier to Francesco von Mendelssohn. The single-storey house, built in a style that crossed the Bauhaus with qualities of his earlier Tunisian retreat, was set in extensive grounds with a small stream. Both the exterior and the interiors provided backdrops for many of his photographs[32]. Two of these are his picture of Jane Fonda taken on the sofa in his sitting room in the short period when she worked as a *Vogue* model before launching her film career (plate 68), and a 1970s shot of artists Gilbert and George set in the loggia (plate 120). Sharing this house and becoming his most enduring companion, collaborator and biographer was the British diplomat and former chargé-d'affaires Valentine Lawford (plate 89). Horst had first met Lawford in New York in 1947, and when work commitments allowed it, they settled together at Oyster Bay, punctuating busy times spent travelling around the world on assignment. This relationship brought a new stability to Horst's life.

ON LOCATION

The 1950s brought two sittings with Jacqueline Bouvier, the future First Lady, the first, shortly before her wedding in 1953 to John F. Kennedy, and the second in 1955 with her sister Lee, later Princess Radziwill (plate 98). The sisters' importance on the social scene was already clear, but Jacky's emergence as style leader and American icon was

Fig.10 Belles of the Gibson Girl Ball (in Mainbocher gowns, from left to right): Miss Wendy Burden, Mrs William S. Paley, Mrs George Abbott and Mrs Philip Isles

just beginning. In 1952, Horst photographed General Dwight D. Eisenhower, shortly to be elected President, with his wife, Mamie, in one of his more engaging compositions (plate 97).

Pictures taken in Europe in the 1950s, away from studio interference from the new *Vogue* editor, had a startling new *plein-air* quality. These ranged from Ian Fleming shot at Kitzbühel (fig.11) to an extended essay on the German conductor Herbert von Karajan (plate 95) in his modern sports car at his Austrian retreat. Karajan looks like a subject out of a science fiction movie in heavyweight contrast to the playful good

Fig. 11 Ian Fleming, Kitzbühel, Austria, 1958

looks of his young wife, Eliette, posed on her bicycle. Horst's first important trip to Austria occurred in 1952, to work on a major advertising campaign with the new model Suzy Parker (plate 106), who would become a major star in the 1960s before attempting a film career[33]. In America that same year, he took his first lifestyle house and interior photographs; the sitter was Consuelo Vanderbilt, Duchess of Marlborough and now Mme Jacques Balsan. This series, encouraged by Diana Vreeland during her time at *Vogue*, was to continue into the 1980s in both *Vogue* and *House and Garden* and was to be collected in the book *Horst: Interiors* by Barbara Plumb (1983). It also provided a platform for collaboration with the urbane and socially adept Lawford, who wrote the accompanying texts.

One of Horst's freshest and most attractive photographs from this decade was taken of the 21-year-old Italian screen actress and 'Miss Italy 1947', Lucia Bosé (plate 93), who was then appearing in a number of neo-realist films, including Cocteau's *Testament of Orpheus*. *Vogue* described Bosé as 'a quiet, lovely, wisp of a girl with street boys' hair'. Horst was introduced to her by his old friend Luchino Visconti, whom he had first photographed in 1935 outside his and Huene's home in Hammamet (plate 29). Then, Visconti had been little more than a playboy, but he had since begun his illustrious film career starting with his work for Jean Renoir. Now he was considering using Bosé in a new film. Horst was so struck by her, that he photographed her immediately. At the same luncheon, Visconti introduced him to Franco Zeffirelli and another friendship developed, but it was not until 1964 that Horst would photograph Zeffirelli in New York (plate 112). Visconti was also responsible for providing the opportunity for Horst to photograph the great Italian novelist Alberto Moravia in Rome in 1957 (plate 94).

The 1960s started well for American *Vogue* with the appointment of the larger-than-life 'Empress of Fashion', Diana Vreeland, as Editor-in-Chief (plate 118). Vreeland served from 1961 until 1971, when a change of approach was deemed necessary. Horst was assigned some of the leading players of the time and produced a number of archetypal images of this energetic decade. His mid-1960s swimwear shoot with Veruschka on location in Hawaii, which filled an entire issue of the June-July 1965 *Vogue Pattern Book*, found the perfect combination of subject, setting and interpretation (plates 107 and 108).

Steve McQueen, on the other hand, was everybody's ideal 1960s man. He made a huge impact in *The Magnificent Seven* (1960), followed by *The Great Escape* (1963), which allowed him to show off his prowess on motorbikes. Now he was in San Francisco about to make one of the best car-chase films of the decade, *Bullitt* (1968). Horst's photograph captures the zeitgeist through McQueen's clothes and pose, high-up in a building with a view over the city (fig.12 and plate 109).

Horst photographed the Windsors surrounded by real and Meissen pugs in 1964 (fig.13), somehow succeeding in keeping up with fashion trends that they had previously led. In Rome, Horst photographed the American painter Cy Twombly, who had settled there in 1957. Twombly was keeping up with the 1960s by raiding the 1920s, the decade they tried to mimic, by wearing a World War I leather greatcoat and driving a restored, very fashionable, 1928 Alfa Romeo sports car (plate 111).

The 1970s remains the decade that good, timeless style overlooked, and work for Horst was necessarily sparse. His portrait of the heavily wrinkled, pipe-smoking W. H. Auden (plate 113), and the more guileful Truman Capote with his sculpted snake accompaniment (plate 119), are two of his best works from this decade. However, Horst's rediscovery by a new group of 1980s style-seeking enthusiasts resulted in increasing commissions. For *Life* magazine, Entertainment Editor James Watters proposed a special issue devoted to the great, but forgotten, Hollywood stars of the 1920s and 1930s.

Horst was commissioned to take nine photographs which appeared in February 1980. This was the most popular issue of *Life* in that year, selling 1.5 million copies. It led to a book contract and continued work with Watters, whose encyclopaedic knowledge of early Hollywood stars made him the ideal interviewer as the two men travelled round America to produce their best-selling book *Return Engagement: Faces to Remember – Then & Now* (1984). The book, which sold 25,000 copies, chronicled the seventy-four sittings that Horst, working with his long-serving assistant Hans Mayr, had taken beginning with a 1979 picture made in Rochester, New York State, of Louise Brooks (plate 114). Hepburn appeared on the cover (plate 115), and other notables included Bette Davis, Lillian Gish and Dorothy Lamour[34].

Return Engagement appeared in the same year as Valentine Lawford's copiously illustrated and definitive biography *Horst: His Work and His World* and the photographer's first major retrospective exhibition at the International Center of Photography, New York. In 1981, Etheleen Staley and Taki Wise had opened their first commercial gallery dedicated to the masters of fashion and style photography in New York with a Horst exhibition which helped to transform his reputation. Richard J.

Fig. 12 Steve McQueen, San Francisco, 1967 (contact sheet)

Tardiff (Rick) took over as his new studio manager and organized the promotion of his work, including print editions and new commissions. Rick would care for Horst for the rest of his life, particularly after the death of Lawford, and become his adopted son and heir. The relaunch of Horst's career was engineered equally successfully in London, through the offices of Andrew Cowan and Hamiltons Gallery in Mayfair. In New York, *Esquire* and the revitalized *Vanity Fair* (which had closed in 1936) were two of many publications that commissioned new work. Raoul Julia was shot by Horst for the former (plate 125). In the late 1970s, French *Vogue* was enjoying one of its golden eras and regularly employed Horst from 1979; his essay on Jerry Hall (plate 131), her then husband Mick Jagger and their two children was taken in the Bahamas[35]. Image-conscious pop stars such as Debbie Harry of Blondie (plate 126) and Duran Duran (plate 132) eagerly sought Horst's timeless elegance while upmarket advertising campaigns led to prestigious sittings with Princess Stephanie of Monaco (plate 123) and Isabella Rossellini (plate 124). Fashion designers including Karl Lagerfeld, Yves Saint-Laurent (whom Horst had photographed regularly since the 1950s), Paloma Picasso (plate 117) and Calvin Klein (plate 122) were all regular subjects both as portrait sitters and in photographs of their creations.

Some of Horst's very last photographs were taken on British assignments, including a 1986 fashion shoot with Yasmin Le Bon. A master class and fashion shoot were organized by Lucinda Chambers at the National Museum of Photography, Film and Television, Bradford, in 1989 with Catherine Bailey (plate 133)[36]. Manolo Blahnik, the internationally esteemed shoe designer, was the subject of one of Horst's last great portraits for *Vogue* in 1990, while his last sitting for British *Vogue* was in 1991 with Princess Michael of Kent, shown against a tapestry background and wearing a family heirloom: a tiara that had belonged to her mother-in-law, Horst's 1934 subject Princess Marina.

Horst's last years were dogged by failing eyesight and poor health, but books and exhibitions proliferated, giving him some comfort that his achievements in the visual arts had made an extraordinary impact.

When Horst died aged ninety-three at his home in Palm Beach Gardens, Florida, on 18

Fig. 13 Duke and Duchess of Windsor, Paris, 1964

November 1999, the obituaries and tributes around the world were lengthy and fulsome[37]. Cathy Horyn in the *New York Times* repaid fellow photographer Eric Boman's adulation – 'Horst really was the 20th century' – while the London *Times* noted that his 'portraits of celebrities, though less well-known, are better pictures' compared to much of his fashion work. *The Times* singled out Horst's 1946 self-portrait shown in a composition with Gertrude Stein as well as his telling portraits of Auden, Moravia and Calvin Klein.

Horst's career can be said to have reached Old Master status when the world's most famous pop goddess, Madonna, created her celebrated hymn to classic fashion photography with her single *Vogue* in 1990. In the video directed by David Fincher, she posed as a recreation of Horst's most iconic fashion image, a model seen from behind, wearing a partially tied, back-laced corset made by Detolle. Horst had taken this photograph in Paris on 11 August 1939 as one of the last images to come out of French *Vogue* before World War II and the German Occupation. Madonna chose it as the essential emblem of fashion photography. Endorsing its inconographic importance to Horst's career, it was featured on the cover of his authorized biography (fig.14)[38]. Horst's fashion photography has been properly celebrated over the past few years with William Ewing's groundbreaking show at the ICP, New York (1984), and more recently at the Musée des Arts de la Mode, Paris (1991). The present volume is the first to be published since Horst's book *Photographs of a Decade* (1944) that is dedicated to his portraiture.

In his approach to portraiture, Horst set out to create a parallel aspirational universe in which his subjects became mysterious and alluring. Bruce Weber, one of many photographers influenced by Horst, artfully described his feelings about Horst's work in a 1992 television documentary: 'The elegance of his photographs … took you to another place, very beautifully … the untouchable quality of the people is really interesting as it gives you something of a distance … it's like seeing somebody from another world … and you wonder who that person is and you really want to know that person and really want to fall in love with that person'[39]. Along with Weber are many other photographers who would cite Horst as an influence including Robert Mapplethorpe, particularly on his flower studies, as did Herb Ritts for his heroic nudes and celebrity portraits[40]. The production by all these photographers, alongside Horst, of large-scale platinum prints in the 1980s promoted the aesthetics of the medium, by introducing a new group of collectors and connoisseurs to the world of art photography.

Gerald Scarfe's 1992 television documentary *Sixty Years and Still in Vogue*, with its tributes by Paloma Picasso, Karl Lagerfeld, Alexander Liberman, Suzy Menkes and Bruce Weber, had neatly summarized in its title the fact that Horst's editorial work could be found almost entirely in one fashion magazine to which he had contributed for nearly the whole of his career. Starting with his first appearance in the pages of *Vogue* in July 1931, it was as one of Huene's anonymous models in a number of

Fig. 14 'Mainbocher Corset', Paris, 1939 (Jacket cover for *Horst: His Work and His World*, Alfred A. Knopf, 1984 and Viking, 1985)

swimwear photographs that Horst made his first impression in the magazine[41]. Then he had the perfect fit and muscled body seen in Huene's torso study idealized at the time (page 203). Over his long lifetime, Horst took on the guise of the urbane, meticulously dressed fashion icon with exemplary manners. He was immediately identifiable in the portraits of Robert Mapplethorpe, Duane Michaels and their many contemporaries. By holding steadfastly to his own ideals and principles of what constituted good taste and style, working with patience and characteristic humility, combined with an unerring eye for composition and psychological insight into his subject matter, Horst, as an artist, remained throughout his life 'Always in Vogue'.

NOTES

1 Personal statement in *Contemporary Photographers* (includes full bibliography and exhibition listing) (Macmillan/St James Press, London, Chicago, 1982, 1988, 1995).

2 The indispensable source of biographical information on Horst is his collaborative book written by Valentine Lawford, *Horst: His Work and His World*, published in l984 after four years of work with the creative input of the Editor at Alfred A. Knopf, Victoria Wilson.

3 Fi McGhee, *Photographers and Their Images* (Conran Octopus, London, 1988), p.84.

4 See also *The Thirties in Vogue* (Octopus Books, London, 1984), p.113.

5 See William A. Ewing, *The Photographic Art of Hoyningen-Huene* (Thames and Hudson, London, 1986) for a full account of his career.

6 *Salute to the Thirties*, foreword by Janet Flanner, (Bodley Head/Viking Press, New York and London, 1971). The book comprises photographs by Horst and George Hoyningen-Huene, and notes on plates by Valentine Lawford. Though undated, a large proportion of Horst's photographs reproduced in this book were taken in the 1940s of personalities who were famous in the 1930s.

7 Though no extant Horst portrait exists of Charles James, one of his early American *Vogue* covers, 15 November 1936, shows off a James ensemble (reproduced in Valerie Lloyd, *The Art of Vogue Photographic Covers*, Octopus Books, London, 1986). The book also reproduces many other Horst covers.

8 Horst's first published photograph appeared, uncredited, in the November 1931 issue of French *Vogue*. It was one of a series of experimental studies he had taken, working with the German-born model Agnetha Fischer. As part of an advertisement, it was used to illustrate the high quality of *Vogue* studio portraiture to entice readers to contact the magazine for a personal sitting with the aim of making the ideal Christmas present.

9 See in particular Steichen's seated portraits of H.G. Wells (1931) or of Winston Churchill (1932).

10 'Miss Lawrence in Widow's crape', American *Vogue*, July 1932, p.40.

11 Kay Francis, American *Vogue*, 1 September 1932, pp.46-7; Bette Davis, *Vanity Fair*, November 1932, p.50; Condé Nast, American *Vogue*, 15 October 1942.

12 French *Vogue*, February 1933, pp.46-7.

13 Horst refers to this approach in *The Art and Techniques of Color Photography* (Simon and Schuster, New York, 1951, p.28): 'I used to be interested in dark subjects, with sharp, beautifully-lit accents – subjects in which the shadows and dark colors blended into dark backgrounds.'

14 See *Esquire*, September 1984, p.144, for Lawford's interview with Horst discussing figures whose style exerted the most influence on Horst's life.

15 Romney Brent first appeared on the London stage in Noël Coward's revue *Words and Music* (1932) but did not perform in the London production of *Conversation Piece*.

16 Toto Koopman in Stiebel silver-grey lamé and Chaumet jewels, 4 April 1934, p.70; Douglas Fairbanks Jnr, 18 April 1934, p.82. The London Season issue of British *Vogue*, 2 May 1934, has a colour photograph cover by Hoyningen-Huene and Horst's four

studies of debutantes: Lady Ursula Manners, Miss Charmain Fain, Lady Gloria Vaughan and Lady Elizabeth Paget on pp.84-5; Viscountess Ridley, 30 May 1934, p.84; Mrs Anthony Eden, 13 June 1934, p.68; Lady Jersey, 17 October 1934, p.62.

17 British *Vogue*, 5 September and 28 November 1934.

18 Amy Fine Collins's important profile 'Reflections of Horst' in *Vanity Fair* (December 1990) with photographs by Eric Boman shows interiors of Horst's house in Oyster Bay and illustrates the full version of the Horst 'gardening' portrait by Beaton.

19 Huene's Hollywood photographs for *Vanity Fair* also appeared in French *Vogue*, July 1934, pp.40-41 and October 1934, pp.86-7.

20 See Robin Gibson and Pamela Roberts, *Madame Yevonde* (National Portrait Gallery, London, 1990).

21 First cover with Lisa Fonssagrives, American *Vogue*, 1 June 1940, followed by 1 September 1940, which both appear subsequently on British editions.

22 Lady Pamela Smith, British *Vogue*, 1935; Frances Farmer, American *Vogue*, 15 November 1939, p.47 and illustrated in Nancy Hall-Duncan, *The History of Fashion Photography* (Alpine Book Company, New York, 1979), p.67.

23 An alternative pose of Crawford in profile showing more of the background of the Roman baths painted by Panini and used in Horst's photographic enlargement for the backdrop was published in American *Vogue*, 1938.

24 Horst gives an amusing account of the sitting in *Portraits of a Decade*, New York, J. J. Augustin, 1944, but misdates the sitting to 1941.

25 American *Vogue*, 15 May 1940, cover.

26 See Suzy Menkes, *The Windsor Style* (Grafton Books, London, 1987) for a fuller account of all Horst's sittings with the Duke and Duchess of Windsor.

27 American *Vogue*, 1941.

28 American *Vogue*, 1 April 1946, pp.156-61.

29 See Carmen's Autobiography, *Staying Beautiful: Beauty Secrets and Attitudes from my Forty Years as a Model*, Carmen and Alfred Allan Lewis (Harper and Row, New York, 1985).

30 American *Vogue*, December 1947, pp.176-9.

31 American *Vogue*, December 1948, p.152.

32 Horst's house in Oyster Bay provides the background for the cover of American *Vogue*, 1 April 1948, the first of many times featured in the pages of *Vogue* and *House and Garden*. See also 'The House That Horst Grew' American *Vogue*, June 1966.

33 See also the colour page of Parker in Austria, British *Vogue*, December 1952.

34 For sittings in California, Horst was assisted by Richard Stanley on the recommendation of George Cukor.

35 French *Vogue*, May 1986.

36 British *Vogue*, August 1989, p.143.

37 *New York Times*, 19 November 1999; *The Times,* the *Daily Telegraph* and *The Independent*, 20 November 1999.

38 Lawford, *Horst: His Work and His World.*

39 *Sixty Years and Still in Vogue*, documentary made by Gerald Scarfe for BBC Omnibus, first broadcast in Britain on 17 November 1992.

40 See Michael Gross, *New York* magazine, 9 September 1991.

41 See French *Vogue*, July 1931, pp.34-5, for two beach studies showing a recognizable Horst. Huene's celebrated diving-board photograph of two models in Izod swimsuits often published as being of Horst can clearly not be of him, as it was published in June 1930, i.e. many months before they met.

Plate 1
Agnetha Fischer, 1931

Plate 2
Mistinguett, Paris, 1933

Plate 3
Mistinguett, Paris, 1933

Plate 4
Francesco von Mendelssohn, Paris, 1931

Plate 5
Alan Pryce-Jones, Paris, 1931

Plate 6
Elsie de Wolfe, Lady Mendl, Paris, 1933

Plate 7
Christian Bérard, Paris, 1933

Plate 8
Cecil Beaton, Paris, 1934

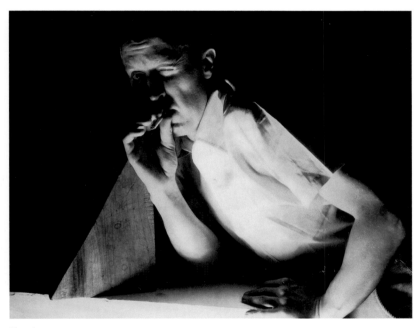

Plate 9
George Hoyningen-Huene, Paris, 1934

Plate 10
Misia Sert, Paris, 1935

Plate 11
Hon. Mrs Reginald 'Daisy' Fellowes, Paris, 1935

Plate 12
Martinez de Hoz, 1935

Plate 13
Tamara Geva, New York, 1936

Plate 14
From left to right: Romney Brent, Noël Coward and Yvonne Printemps for *Conversation Piece*, 1933

Plate 15
Noël Coward, 1933

Plate 16
Noël Coward and Gertrude Lawrence in *Tonight at 8.30,* 1936

Plate 17
Gertrude Lawrence, New York, 1936

Plate 18
HRH Princess Marina of Greece, Paris, 1934

Plate 19
Princess Karam of Kapurthala, 1934

Plate 20
Merle Oberon, 1930s

Plate 21
Lily Pons, Paris, 1933

Plate 22
Elsa Schiaparelli, Paris, 1937

Plate 23
Valentina, New York, 1936

Plate 24
Merle Oberon, London, 1934

Plate 25
Tilly Losch, 1939

Plate 26
Oliver Messel, Hollywood, 1935

Plate 27
Katharine Hepburn, Hollywood, 1935

Plate 28
Helena Kuo, New York, 1942

Plate 29
Luchino Visconti (Count Visconti di Modrone), Hammamet, Tunisia 1935

Plate 30
Helen Bennett, 1936

Plate 31
Helen Bennett, 1936

Plate 32
Gabrielle (Coco) Chanel, Paris, 1937

Plate 33
Duchess of Windsor, Paris, 1937

Plate 34
Olivia de Havilland, New York, 1936

Plate 35
Deanna Durbin, 1936

Plate 36
Margaret Rawlings, New York, 1935

Plate 37
Ginger Rogers, New York, 1936

Plate 38
Eve Curie, 1938

Plate 39
Eve Curie, 1937

Plate 40
Bette Davis, New York, 1939

Plate 41
Joan Crawford, New York, 1938

Plate 42
Ethel Waters in *Mamba's Daughters*, 1939

Plate 43
Emlyn Williams in *Night Must Fall*, New York, 1935

Plate 44
Barbara Hutton, Countess Haugwitz-Reventlow, New York, 1939

Plate 45
Sylvia, Lady Ashley, Mrs Douglas Fairbanks Snr, 1938

Plate 46
Lud, Paris, 1938

Plate 47
Jessica Tandy, New York, 1938

Plate 48
Gary Cooper and his wife 'Rocky' Veronica Balfe, 1938

Plate 49
Janet Gaynor and her husband Adrian, 1940

Plate 50
Ingrid Bergman and Burgess Meredith in *Liliom*, New York, 1940

Plate 51
Veronica Lake, New York, 1941

Plate 52
Merle Oberon, New York, 1942

Plate 53
Myrna Loy, New York, 1942

Plate 54
Marlene Dietrich, New York, 1942

Plate 55
Marlene Dietrich, New York, 1942

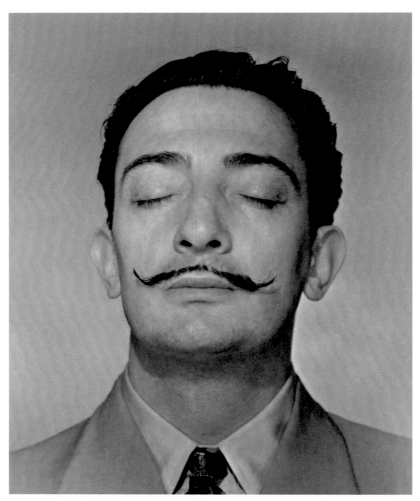

Plate 56
Salvador Dalí, New York, 1943

Plate 57
Leonor Fini, Paris, 1946

Plate 58
Duchess of Windsor, New York, 1943

Plate 59
Duchess of Windsor, New York, 1947

Plate 60
Arturo Toscanini, New York, 1940

Plate 61
Alicia Markova, New York, 1941

Plate 62
Gene Tierney, New York, 1941

Plate 63
Muriel Maxwell, New York, 1940

64a

64b

64c

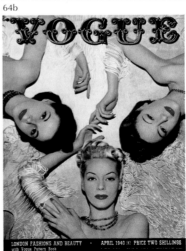

64d

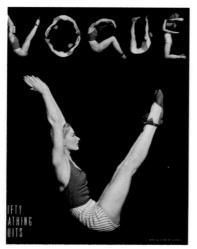

64e   64f

Plate 64
American and British *Vogue* covers (original tear sheets)
a. Bettina Bollegard, 1 November 1941
b. Muriel Maxwell, 1 August 1940
c. Helen Bennett, 15 May 1938
d. Helen Bennett, April 1940
e. Lisa Fonssagrives, 1 June 1940
f. Lisa Fonssagrives, 1 September 1940

Plate 65
Helen Hayes in *Twelfth Night*, New York, 1940

Plate 66
Paulette Goddard, New York, 1941

Plate 67
Loretta Young, New York, 1941

Plate 68
Jane Fonda, New York, 1959

Plate 69
Edith Sitwell, New York, 1948

Plate 70
Lily Cushing, Mrs William T. Emmet, New York, 1942

Plate 71
Tallulah Bankhead in *The Eagle Has Two Heads*, New York, 1947

Plate 72
Tallulah Bankhead in *The Little Foxes,* New York, 1939

Plate 73
Lisa Fonssagrives, New York, 1940

Plate 74
Gloria Vanderbilt, New York, 1941

Plate 75
Milada Mladova, New York, 1939

Plate 76
Carmen Dell'Orefice, New York, 1947

Plate 77
Lady Diana Cooper, New York, 1940

Plate 78
Millicent Rogers, New York, 1938

Plate 79
Rita Hayworth, New York, 1947

Plate 80
Tallulah Bankhead, New York, 1940s

Plate 81
Olivier Messiaen, Paris, 1946

Plate 82
Gertrude Stein, Paris, 1946

Plate 83
Jean Cocteau, Venice, 1947

Plate 84
Misia Sert, Venice, 1947

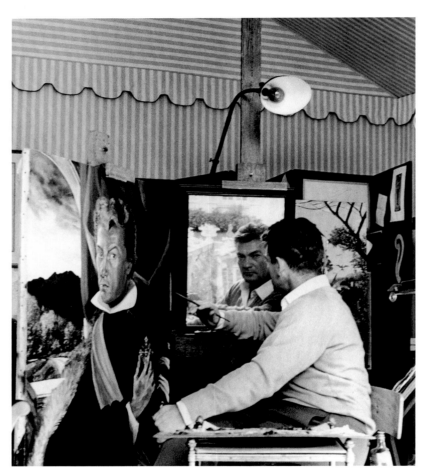

Plate 85
Jean Marais, 1950s

Plate 86
Diamante Boschetti, Venice, 1947

Plate 87
Carlos Chavez, Mexico, 1946

Plate 88
Montage including Diego Rivera, Mexico, 1941

Plate 89
Valentine Lawford, Dorset, England, 1948

Plate 90
Sir Osbert Sitwell, 1948

Plate 91
Lisa Fonssagrives, 1951

Plate 92
Irving Penn, New York, 1951

Plate 93
Lucia Bosé, Rome 1952

Plate 94
Alberto Moravia, Rome, 1957

Plate 95
Herbert von Karajan, Kitzbühel, Austria, 1958

Plate 96
Eliette von Karajan, Kitzbühel, Austria, 1958

Plate 97
Dwight D. Eisenhower and his wife Mamie (Geneva Doud), 1952

Plate 98
Jacqueline Bouvier Kennedy and her sister Lee Radziwill, New York, 1955

Plate 99
Maria Callas, New York, 1952

Plate 100
Princess Colonna, Rome, 1952

Plate 101
Dame Sybil Thorndike and Sir Lewis Casson in *The Potting Shed*, New York, 1957

Plate 102
Katina Paxinou in *Electra*, Athens, 1955

Plate 103
Louise de Vilmorin, Verriers, France, 1958

Plate 104
Ingrid Bergman, Paris, 1959

Plate 105
Mme Jacques Balsan (Consuelo Vanderbilt, Duchess of Marlborough), Oyster Bay, Long Island, 1952

Plate 106
Suzy Parker, Kitzbühel, Austria, 1952

Plate 107
Veruschka, Hawaii, 1965

Plate 108
Veruschka, Hawaii, 1965

Plate 109
Steve McQueen, San Francisco, 1967

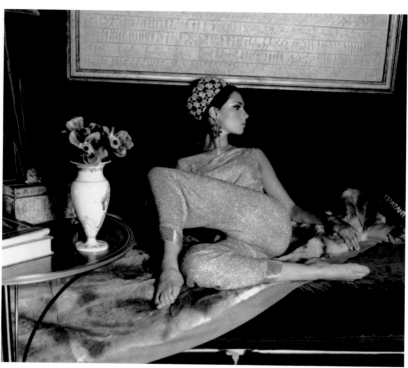

Plate 110
Jennifer O'Neill, 1964

Plate 111
Cy Twombly, Rome, 1966

Plate 112
Franco Zeffirelli, New York, 1964

Plate 113
W. H. Auden, New York, 1970

Plate 114
Louise Brooks, Rochester, New York, 1979

Plate 115
Katharine Hepburn, New York, 1981

Plate 116
Arthur Miller, 1980

Plate 117
Paloma Picasso, New York, 1979

Plate 118
Diana Vreeland, New York, 1979

Plate 119
Truman Capote, 1977

Plate 120
Gilbert and George, Oyster Bay, Long Island, 1970s

Plate 121
Roy Lichtenstein, New York, 1978

Plate 122
Calvin Klein, New York, 1984

Plate 123
Princess Stephanie of Monaco, New York, 1985

Plate 124
Isabella Rossellini, 1984

Plate 125
Raoul Julia, New York, 1982

Plate 126
Debbie Harry, 1988

Plate 127
Erté, Barbados, 1986

Plate 128
Bruce Weber, New York, 1988

Plate 129
Kerry Harper, New York, 1980

Plate 130
Karl Lagerfeld, 1980

Plate 131
Jerry Hall, Barbados, 1986

Plate 132
Duran Duran, London, 1986

Plate 133
Catherine Bailey, Bradford, England, 1989

NOTES ON PLATES

A few errors of dating have been adjusted after checking with other published sources such as the three editions of *Vogue*. Where known, actual sitting dates have been provided, as well as the publication date, which usually tends to be three months after sitting.

Plate 1, AGNETHA FISCHER

Horst's first published photograph appeared uncredited in a bold advertisement in French *Vogue* offering the magazine's readers a rare chance to obtain a most 'seductive Christmas present' in the form of a signed *Vogue* studio portrait of themselves that would 'resemble in quality those they normally admired in the magazine each month'. It is unknown whether the offer was taken up, but this image of the German model Agnetha Fischer is an early foretaste of the Horst style in its classic linear and graphic composition. Fischer was also one of Huene's favourite models with whom Horst also worked on occasions, including a session when he photographed her with Toto Koopman. Fischer later became a photographer for French *Vogue*.
Published: French *Vogue*, November 1931, p.59

Plate 2, MISTINGUETT (1875-1956)

Born Jeanne-Marie Florentine Bourgeois, 'Miss' made her stage debut in 1893 at the Casino de Paris and rapidly became the undisputed queen of *fin-de-siècle* music hall, often appearing in light comedy and musical plays at the Moulin Rouge, which she part owned. Her stage name was a shortened version of 'Miss' and 'guingette' the name by which popular dance halls, favoured by the French working classes, were known. Aged fifty-eight when Horst took this portrait she would continue to perform until a final performance in New York in 1951. Mistinguett was said to have had the most beautiful legs in the world and they were insured for a million francs.
Taken: Paris, 21 December 1933
Published: French *Vogue*, February 1934, p.33

Plate 3, MISTINGUETT (1875-1956)

Horst's photographic session with Mistinguett was taken to publicize her new revue *Folies en Folies* that was staged at the Folies-Bergère and introduced her second most famous song (after *Mon Homme*) *C'est Vrai* written by Albert Willemetz and later favoured by drag artists impersonating her act. Her protégé, who was also the love of her life and co-starred with her in the 1910s, was Maurice Chevalier, whose career she helped launch. Normally appearing at the Casino de Paris, she was unable to do so at this time as her rival Cecile Sorel was ensconced there with her hit revue *Vive Paris*. Mistinguett was a much-loved French institution and Jean Cocteau claimed that her distinctive voice affected him as bagpipes do a Scotsman.
Taken: Paris, 21 December 1933

Plate 4, FRANCESCO VON MENDELSSOHN

A descendant of the composer Felix Mendelssohn-Bartholdy and a distinguished cellist (he performed on his ancestor's Stradivarius), Francesco was also a theatre producer in pre-war Germany. He brought Noël Coward's plays, in particular *Private Lives* and *Bitter Sweet*, to the Berlin stage and also staged some of Brecht's work. With his sister Eleonora, Mendelssohn emigrated to the United States as Hitler seized power. Mendelssohn's collection of paintings included works by Rembrandt, El Greco, Goya and other Old Masters as well as paintings by Picasso. In reduced circumstances in New York, Horst lent his friend $5000. At Mendelssohn's insistence, he received the Stradivarius as collateral, replaced in time by a Picasso. Though he could well afford to pay back the loan, Mendelssohn let him keep it in return for his kindness. Horst sold it years later (with a Toulouse-Lautrec) as a down-payment for real estate at Oyster Bay.
Taken: *Vogue* studio, Paris, 10 December 1931

Plate 5, ALAN PRYCE-JONES (1908-2000)

Alan Pryce-Jones was a distinguished historian and man of letters, photographed here at the outset of his career. His novel *The Pink Danube* had just been published. Fifteen years later he would become a celebrated editor of *The Times Literary Supplement* but here he is posed, aged twenty-three, in a slightly louche, dandified pose. This arrangement is typical of Horst's early male portraits and the style – borrowed from Huene – is recognizable in his photograph of Cole Porter and most markedly in that of William Etting, taken in Paris in the same year.
Taken: *Vogue* studio, Paris, 1931

Plate 6, ELSIE DE WOLFE, LADY MENDL (1865-1950)

Once an actress, American-born Elsie de Wolfe became the hostess *ne plus ultra* on both sides of the Atlantic. After her marriage to Sir Charles Mendl, Press Counsellor at the British Embassy, she settled in Paris, becoming the most successful interior decorator of her day. She advocated a return to the French 'high' style of the nineteenth century, but as Lawford remarked, for a while 'her name became synonymous with a taste for beige'. It is said that after climbing the Acropolis, she remarked 'My color!' For Horst, she poses beneath her Boldini portrait, painted in 1905, when as a young lady she acquired an old house near the Trianon, Versailles. She restored it and ran it as a hospital in World War I (for which she received the Croix de Guerre). Horst and Lawford met many of the fashionable Parisian *monde* through her lavish entertaining, though she could not abide 'intellectuals'. She was famously reticent about her birth date (although proud of her presentation to Queen Victoria in 1884), and one of her endearing habits was to stand on her head daily to ensure the endurance of her youthful looks. *Vogue* applauded her 'incisive taste, her abounding elastic vitality'.
Taken: Paris, 1933
Published: American *Vogue*, 1 October 1933, p.42

Plate 7, CHRISTIAN BÉRARD (1902-49)

Christian 'Bébé' Bérard was skilled in many branches of the fine and applied arts, from set design for Cocteau among others, to portrait painting, fabric and interior design and, most enduringly, fashion illustration for *Vogue*. The magazine snatched him from a rival, not because it liked his work – Condé Nast could not abide his faceless drawings – but for his other skill as a barometer for what was new in the cultural life of Paris. *Vogue* called him 'a True Bohemian, impulsive, unpunctual, untidy and ready to sit all night at a café in a passionate discussion of art'. His movable garden set for Jouvet's production of *L'Ecole des Femmes* was groundbreaking. Memorable too were his designs for *The Madwoman of Chaillot* and the ballets *Cotillon* and *The Seventh Symphony*. He had been Vuillard's favourite pupil and his neo-Romanticism was an antidote to the formalistic rigour of the incipient Bauhaus style, and was influential on the designs of Elsa Schiaparelli and the first collection of Christian Dior. The *Vogue* editor who poached him never really understood him: 'He used the ladies' room at the office, but you could hardly call what went on there washing up. He just went in and threw paint about ... He was not orderly'. She also lamented that 'his black beard was full of spaghetti and little active pets who lodged there ...'
Taken: Painting a screen for Edward Molyneux, Paris, 1933

Plate 8, CECIL BEATON (1904-80)

Both *Vogue* photographers, Horst and Cecil Beaton appeared to have had a rivalry that lasted their entire professional lives. Beaton was a friend and colleague of Huene and it is likely that he was resentful of Huene's affectionate regard of the young German. Beaton never missed an opportunity to belittle Horst publicly. In 1930 Huene and Horst stayed with Beaton at his house, Ashcombe, and the visit is vividly recalled in Horst's biography. Horst spoke almost no English but was obliged to play the parlour game 'Charades' and to act out the word 'quaint': he threw his arms and legs around for what seemed like an eternity of misery and embarrassment until he was let off the hook. Beaton, whom he suspected of having engineered the incident, found it irresistibly funny. When Horst assumed the role of Paris *Vogue*'s Chief Photographer, Beaton was almost apoplectic and remained so for decades. On a visit to Oyster Bay, he wasted little time in criticizing his host's taste. In 1971 Horst praised him lavishly in the book *Salute to the Thirties* – his set and costume design, his portraits, his fashion photographs, his sittings with the Royal Family, his authorship of diaries and of a play, his draughtsmanship – all masterpieces according to Horst. However, he illustrated the encomium with two photographs: one taken in 1936, of which Horst said 'I wanted him to look like Garbo in Queen Christina' (Beaton had had an abortive affair with the actress, which was then generally unknown); the other in drag at a fancy-dress ball as the novelist Elinor Glyn taken by Huene – and beyond parody. Unsurprisingly Beaton was stung into giving the book a bad review in the English press. In Beaton's book on the history of photography, *The Magic Image* (1975), the success of Horst's œuvre is laid squarely at the feet of Huene.
Taken: Paris, 1934

Plate 9, GEORGE HOYNINGEN-HUENE (1900-68)

Termed 'volatile' in every biography, Huene was born in St Petersburg; his father was the Chief Equerry to the last Tsar, and his mother was the daughter of the American ambassador to the Imperial Russian Court. Horst said this of his mentor: 'By this time George had given up being photographed as a gentleman. He had been in Hollywood and seen how the people who worked there dressed. This picture shows his first attempt to look like an American movie director (and shortly after this he began his first movie)'. Horst became his protégé, occasional model and assistant and taught himself to photograph in the elegant, fluid Huene style. By 1935, Horst had made himself indispensable in the *Vogue* Paris studios, having made numerous portrait and fashion pictures independently of his mentor (with whom he now lived). In the same year, Huene disputed a clause in his *Vogue* contract and at lunch with the visiting Art Director of American *Vogue*, Dr Agha, became so incensed that it is said he up-ended their lunch table and walked out of the restaurant and *Vogue* (where he had been Chief Photographer since the mid-1920s). Huene went to *Vogue*'s rival, *Harper's Bazaar*, and Horst took his place at French *Vogue*. In time, Huene became a consultant on the films of George Cukor and an inspiring teacher of photography, settling permanently in Hollywood. On his death, he left his archive of photographs to Horst, who had learnt so much from them in his formative years.
Taken: Paris, 1934

Plate 10, MISIA SERT (1872-1950)

Born in St Petersburg to a Polish family of artists, Misia Sert was a talented pianist whose greatest legacy was inspiring others to create. Married three times she was painted on many occasions by Renoir, Vuillard, Bonnard and Toulouse-Lautrec. These portraits can be seen in the world's major museums. Sert brought Diaghilev and Stravinsky together. She also inspired two characters in Proust's *Remembrance of Things Past* as well as 'discovering' the design genius of Coco Chanel. In the 1930s Sert promoted the work of her third husband, the Spanish painter and muralist José-Maria Sert.
Taken: In Ira Belline black silk pyjamas for the Hon. Mrs Reginald Fellowes' Le Bal Oriental, Paris, 1935
Published: French *Vogue*, August 1935, p.27; American *Vogue*, 15 August 1935, p.35

Plate 11, HON. MRS REGINALD 'DAISY' FELLOWES (1887-1962)

Despite her title and the nickname 'Daisy', Mrs Fellowes was not English at all. The daughter of a Franco-Danish duke and an American mother, of the Singer family, she was born Marguerite Decazes de Glücksbierg. Her first husband was Prince Jean de Broglie. She was beautiful, rich, clever and ruthless, a much-photographed icon of her times. At one point she was the Editor-at-Large in Paris for the Condé Nast publications and much admired by a generation of *Vogue* photographers (De Meyer, Beaton, Huene and Steichen took her likeness). Her barbed and cruel *bons mots* were as accurate as they were original, despite, as Lawford remembers, being

'uttered in a casual tone and a curiously small and thin and high-pitched voice'. Between the wars she was a renowned hostess and here she is photographed in the costume for Le Bal Oriental she held in Paris in 1935. She possessed an inventive, if macabre, sense of humour, according to Lawford, once inviting her pet hates with their own *bêtes noires* to a dinner of beer, sausages and sauerkraut. She wore black to be presented at court and crossed herself each time she passed an advertisement for Singer Sewing Machines (the source of her wealth). When there was someone else in her favourite cinema seat, she simply sat on top of them. On the fall of France she escaped with her daughter and husband to England. Her daughter became a V.A.D. nurse, her husband joined the Home Guard while Daisy became the First President of the new Incorporated Society of London Fashion Designers promoting British fashions and fabrics.
Taken: Dressed for Le Bal Oriental, with lacquered hair by Antoine, Paris, 1935
Published: French *Vogue*, August 1935, p.15 (variant pose); American *Vogue*, 15 August 1935

Plate 12, MARTINEZ DE HOZ

According to Horst and Lawford, Madame Martinez de Hoz was a well-known member of a coterie of South American émigrés, based in Paris before the war. She was also a fixture on the costume ball, *fête-champêtre* and *tableau vivant* circuit and appears in this photograph as Watteau's *Gilles* for Count Etienne de Beaumont's 'Masterpieces of Paintings' ball of 1935. Horst also photographed Madame Jean Larivière, wife of an Argentinian diplomat, as Goya's *Mayas on a Balcony* at the same ball. Fifteen years later, both ladies appeared again in *Vogue* as attendees of yet another de Beaumont ball. The women had been asked to come 'beautiful and adorned; the men to come in white gloves'. There was dancing in the de Beaumonts' large white and gilt ballroom under a gigantic Picasso mural *The Ball*. Aside from the social pages, Mme de Hoz was no stranger to the fashion pages of *Vogue*. In 1947 she modelled hats with other South American ladies for the camera of André Ostier.
Taken: Mme de Hoz as *Gilles* at the Beaumont Ball, 4 July 1935
Published: American *Vogue*, 15 August 1935, p.37

Plate 13, TAMARA GEVA (1907-97)

This portrait of Tamara Geva and her young attendant was taken as part of a two-page advertisement for Bergdorf Goodman, the famous Manhattan department store in 1936. A dancer in musicals, plays and films, Geva is best known for her role as Vera Baranova, a dancehall girl, in Rodgers and Hart's show *On Your Toes* (1936). It was choreographed by George Balanchine, who first met her in St Petersburg in the early 1920s at the Maryinsky Theatre School, where he was a ballroom dance tutor and she a pupil. They married shortly afterwards (she was fifteen years old, he was three years her senior) and to earn a living, the newly weds danced for privately arranged shows and sang and played piano at nightclubs. In 1924, allowed to leave Russia temporarily, they embarked on an unsuccessful tour of Germany and came to London for a two-week appearance at the Empire, Leicester Square. Recalled to Russia, they decided instead to defect and

travelled to Paris, where they auditioned for the Diaghilev Ballets Russes. Geva appeared with Anton Dolin in *Le Train Bleu*. Her and Balanchine's marriage dissolved amicably and her former husband continued to create roles for her in musicals and in his own American Ballet company. She appeared in Florenz Ziegfeld's *Whoopee!* (1928) and after *On Your Toes*, concentrated on theatre work and films. The latter included *Their Big Moment* (1934), *Orchestra Wives* (1942) and the choreography for *Specter of the Rose* (1946). Her portrait by Horst shares similarities with one taken four years earlier by Huene of Iya, Lady Abdy at Le Bal Oriental in Paris. In that photograph, Horst himself played the young man with sunshade.
Taken: New York, 1936
Published: Delman design for Bergdorf Goodman advertisement, American *Vogue*, 1 November 1936, p.5

Plate 14, (left to right) ROMNEY BRENT (1902-76), NOËL COWARD (1899-1973) and YVONNE PRINTEMPS (1894-1977)

'It would be hard', observed *Vogue*, 'to combine three more versatile and civilised creatures'. Dubbing Coward 'the Wonder Boy of English literature', he is flanked by 'two brilliant players', Yvonne Printemps and the Mexican-American actor Romney Brent to make up the cast and provide 'a most witty and fruitful trilogy' in Coward's Regency-set operetta. Brent, the son a diplomat, was educated and brought up in Paris, London, New York and Mexico. As well as directing and appearing in numerous plays on the London and Broadway stage he also had a film career. As a playwright, he collaborated on a musical of *Nymph Errant* with Cole Porter for Gertrude Lawrence. Printemps, the partner of Sasha Guitry, had worked with Coward before, appearing in a revue at the British Embassy Ball in Paris, but this was to be her first English-speaking leading role in London. Subsequently Horst photographed her again in London in her *Conversation Piece* costume for pictures that appeared in *Vanity Fair* and British *Vogue*. In this photograph Printemps wears an outfit by Lanvin.
Taken: *Conversation Piece* group, 1933
Published: British *Vogue*, January 1934, p.46; American *Vogue*, February 1934, p.30

Plate 15, NOËL COWARD (1899-1973)

According to Lawford's biography Horst first met Coward at 11am, in the bar of the Ritz in Paris, one summer's day after a long all-night photography session. 'I asked if I could photograph him. "Don't pose so much! Look at me!" Actors! Theatre people always know what the best angle is and I wanted to get him out of that.'
Taken: 1933; published Paris, 1935

Plate 16, NOËL COWARD (1899-1973) and GERTRUDE LAWRENCE (1898-1952)

Lawrence and Coward were the most popular double act on the English stage in the 1930s and later went on to conquer America. This photograph captures them as they appeared in the revue *Tonight at 8.30* (formerly known as *Tonight at 7.30*). In Lawrence, Coward found his equal and he wrote the part of Amanda in *Private Lives* with only her in mind. Their relationship could at times be described as 'stormy' but, as Lawford noted, this made 'all the more entertaining and endearing the flawless precision and professionalism of their give-and-take on stage'.

Taken: On the set of *Tonight at 8.30*; design by Gladys Calthrop, 1936

Plate 17, GERTRUDE LAWRENCE (1898-1952)

Horst's very first portrait of an actress was of Gertrude Lawrence, taken several years earlier than this photograph. She had just starred in Noël Coward's *Private Lives* to great acclaim in New York (1931). Horst had posed her on a zebra-skin rug, which was considered rather daring. He said of her, 'She knew more about dresses than I did – she knew how to stand and move'. Apart from her successes with Noël Coward – he provided her with her best roles – she was triumphant in the musicals *Lady in the Dark* (1941) and *The King and I* with Yul Brynner (1951). Lawford believes that in this informal picture, taken in her dressing room between set-ups, '[Horst] captures her as she was at her most natural, irresistible and unforgettable: at the peak of her health and happiness and already at the height of her fame'.

Taken: In her dressing room between acts of *Tonight at 8.30*, New York, 1936

Published: American *Vogue*, January 1937, p.54

Plate 18, HRH PRINCESS MARINA OF GREECE (1906-68)

British *Vogue*'s 'Royal Wedding Number' of November 1934 marked the first occasion that a portrait of a royal princess appeared in *Vogue* taken by a fashion photographer, and Horst found her enchanting. The sitter was Princess Marina of Greece, daughter of Prince Nicholas of Greece and Grand Duchess Helene Vladimirovna of Russia, betrothed to The Duke of Kent, youngest surviving son of George V and Queen Mary. 'Princess Marina', ran the caption accompanying eight photographs, 'posed specially in the *Vogue* studio for Mr Horst, who took all the lovely pictures'. *Vogue* trumpeted their union as 'The first all-royal wedding of a king's son in England since 1795' but it lasted barely eight years; the Duke was posted as missing in action in 1942. The Duchess of Kent became a much-loved member of the Royal Family and the model for princesses of the modern age to follow.

Taken: *Vogue* studio, Paris, 1934

Published: British *Vogue*, 28 November 1934, p.77

Plate 19, PRINCESS KARAM OF KAPURTHALA

A fixture on the social scene in the pre- and post-war years, the Princess was in demand as a *Vogue* model, frequently for jewellery stories like this one for Horst and for others by Cecil Beaton (who photographed her in a diamond bracelet by Cartier, emblazoned with an emerald 'the size of a small fruit'). *Vogue* marvelled at the Princess's hands-on approach to party giving: 'Not long ago she went to a friend's house in Paris and prepared all the food herself for a big party – most surprising for she doesn't look the sort who could do it, being one of the most exquisite creatures of our time.' Shortly before the war, she demonstrated her noted sense of practicality at

Lady Mendl's circus-themed ball, where guests wondered why there were no elephants at the 'big top'. 'These elephants', reported *Vogue*, 'caused more speculation and gossip than any beautiful woman ... The true story is that Princess Karam, the only person who knew how ladies should ride elephants, tried one out, with her hotel bed-mattress strapped to an elephant's back. The circus elephant was not educated in Indian elegance and trod down half the circus in protestation'. Lady Mendl dropped the elephants after that.

Taken: 27 April 1934

Published: French *Vogue*, June 1934, p.48; American *Vogue*, 15 June 1934, p.48; British *Vogue*, 11 July 1934, p.55

Plate 20, MERLE OBERON (1911-79)

In this fashion sitting for *Vogue*, Horst has constructed one of his elaborate sets out of hardboard and enhanced it with photographic enlargements of Piranesian-type architectural details to create a dark cave-like set with which to enhance Oberon's dark features. Although unpublished, it was typical of much of Horst's 1930s fashion work that resulted from his collaboration with set designer Jacques Emilio Terry. Once established as an important screen presence Alexander Korda, her screen mentor, sold part of her film contract to Sam Goldwyn so that Oberon began commuting between London and Hollywood. For her second American film, *The Dark Angel* (1935), she was nominated for an Academy Award. As a result of a near-fatal car crash in 1937 the filming of *I, Claudius* with Charles Laughton and director Josef von Sternberg had to be cancelled, but her career subsequently revived and in 1939 she played opposite Laurence Olivier as Cathy Linton in *Wuthering Heights* and continued to make films until her last film – *Interval* (1973) – which she also produced and co-edited.

Taken: 1930s

Plate 21, LILY PONS (1904-76)

The French-born diva Lily Pons transcended the relatively narrow world of opera to reach audiences on a dramatic scale. She was for a time one of the most famous women in the world. She starred in Hollywood films, thrilled audiences at the Metropolitan Opera House, was a frontline entertainer for United States troops overseas and a front rank fashion icon, her image appearing regularly in French and American *Vogue*. Seldom off the Best Dressed lists of the 1940s, *Vogue* reported that she had time on her return journey from performing to GIs to acquire some of the first couture clothes made after Paris was liberated. Her films, mostly about opera singers, including *I Dream Too Much* (1935) and *Hitting a New High* (1937), made full use of her dazzling coloratura soprano. Such was the esteem in which she was held, that a town in Maryland named itself Lilypons in her honour and is well known today for its water gardens. For an anniversary of her birth, it cultivated a special water lily with a hundred leaves. Locomotives were also named in her honour and she appeared on the cover of *Time* magazine at least twice. Pons shone particularly in Indian dress in Délibes' *Lakmé* and also in Rimsky-Korsakov's *Le Coq d'Or*, both of which the Metropolitan Opera revived especially for

her, and in Donizetti's *Lucia di Lammermoor*. She married the conductor André Kostelanetz and in 1997 she was the subject of a commemorative stamp issued by the US postal service.
Taken: *Vogue* studio, Paris, 2 June 1933
Published: French *Vogue*, August 1933 (uncredited); American *Vogue*, April 1935, p.70

Plate 22, ELSA SCHIAPARELLI (1890-1973)
Horst met the celebrated and innovative couturière at her Paris home on the rue Barbet-de-Jouy, where dinner was served on square black plates. Later she acquired the house of Princess Mathilde, niece of Napoleon. Schiaparelli was Chanel's only real competitor and they loathed each other. Chanel caught Horst lunching with her rival ('That Italian artist who makes dresses') and Horst, having risen to greet her, was kept on his feet as she talked to him for an hour, his lunch companion ignored. Schiaparelli was the only leading designer who was not French; she came from a Roman family with a long tradition of scholarship (one member discovered the canals of Mars, another the first tomb of the Valley of the Kings) and she had studied philosophy. Schiaparelli is known for her surreal and witty fantasies, her invention of the colour 'Shocking Pink', her distaste for buttons (preferring studs and zippers), her 'shoe' hat and her Dalí-decorated dresses with lobster motifs. Schiaparelli visited Huene and Horst in Tunisia, where she received lessons on the Bedouin art of draping fabric without stitching. The austerity of the war years effectively ended her career and in 1954 she closed her boutique doors, removing the stuffed bear, painted 'shocking pink' by Dalí, with drawers in its stomach, and 'Pascal', a larger than life-size artist's wooden dummy.
Taken: Paris, 1937
Published: American *Vogue*, 1 September 1937, p.97

Plate 23, VALENTINA (1904-89)
The sculptural fashion creations of Valentina (Mrs George Schlee) were not practicable, being steeped in the heritage of her Russian roots and designed for maximum impact rather than wearability. Originally an actress, her family fled from Kiev to Paris during the Russian Revolution, and from there Valentina reached New York. She established a clothes shop in 1928 and her clientele included society women and actresses, among them Greta Garbo, Lynn Fontanne and Claudette Colbert. She also designed for films and theatre. She was saluted in a popular song by Comden and Green: 'Valentina's where I've been/I just adore Val ...' Valentina and her husband George Schlee introduced Horst to their close friend Garbo and he remembered weekends spent with the three of them in Connecticut: 'Once Garbo knocked at my door at six in the morning and said, "Let's go for a walk, let's look at the frogs".'
Taken: New York, 1936

Plate 24, MERLE OBERON (1911-79)
The beautiful dark-haired leading lady of British and Hollywood films was born in India, in Bombay, where she spent her early years. Her father was a railway engineer from Darlington and her mother was Eurasian. Anxious to obscure her origins, she claimed throughout her life to have been born in Tasmania. Born Estelle Merle O'Brien Thompson she arrived in London, aged seventeen, working first as a café hostess under the name Queenie O'Brien. Oberon entered films as an extra in 1930 before being spotted and groomed for stardom by the producer and director Alexander Korda (her husband between 1939 and 1945). She played Anne Boleyn in the highly successful *The Private Life of Henry VIII* (1933) and is here photographed during the production of another Korda directed film *The Private Life of Don Juan* (1934) in which she appeared with Douglas Fairbanks Snr. Her nephew Michael Korda, the publishing executive, wrote a controversial novel partially based on her life, entitled *Queenie*.
Taken: London, September 1934

Plate 25, TILLY LOSCH (1907-75)
An exquisite Viennese beauty, Losch was much photographed by Beaton, Horst and Huene and her likeness was painted by Bérard and Oliver Messel. Her charms and impetuosity were apparently a heady, irresistible mix. Edward James, the collector and patron of Surrealists, fell for her after her wordless performance as a medieval nun in Max Rheinhardt's *The Miracle* (Diana Cooper played the Madonna). Their marriage was tempestuous, their divorce a scandal – he sued *her*, which was, for the times, unthinkable. A dancer and mime artist, she masked her technical inexperience with a shimmering stage presence, having started her career at the Vienna Opera School. She danced her first solo in the presence of Richard Strauss. In an effort to salvage his ailing marriage, James bought his wife her own ballet company, Les Ballets, in 1933 and commissioned for her *The Seven Deadly Sins* by Brecht, Weill and Balanchine, as well as a Tchelitchew-designed production of *Errante*. Losch transferred her *Mitteleuropaisch* allure to films with her dancing; as an Arabian houri in *The Garden of Allah* (1936), starring Marlene Dietrich, and in the Western *Duel in the Sun* (1946), as *Vogue* described it, 'with the blazing abandon of a Roman candle'. Horst took this portrait in the year she remarried and became the Countess of Carnarvon.
Taken: 1939

Plate 26, OLIVER MESSEL (1904-78)
Oliver Messel is regarded as one of the leading set designers for the stage, opera and films that Britain has ever produced. He was for a time the most highly paid designer in the world; his creations regarded as romantic and magical but eminently practical. His film work included costumes for Alexander Korda's *The Private Life of Don Juan* (1934) and the following year for *The Scarlet Pimpernel*, Michael Powell's *The Thief of Baghdad* (1940) and Joseph L. Mankiewicz's *Suddenly Last Summer* (1959), for which he was nominated for an Oscar. He also designed *Sleeping Beauty* for the Royal Ballet and the re-opening of the Royal Opera House after the war. For the stage his many triumphs included *Ring Around the Moon* (1950), the opera *Idomeneo* (1951), revived four times, and *The House of Flowers* (1954). His good looks and easy charm made him a fixture on the social circuit and for British *Vogue*. He was one

of the most photographed male figures of his time, having been a sitter for, among others, Cecil Beaton, Clifford Coffin, Norman Parkinson and his much adored nephew Tony Armstrong-Jones (later Lord Snowdon), as well as Huene and Horst. He was among the guests at Cecil Beaton's house when the host humiliated Horst on his first visit to England (see p.178). Horst was put out of his misery by Messel and they became great friends. This photograph was taken in Hollywood, where Messel was co-designing costumes and sets for George Cukor's *Romeo and Juliet*.
Taken: Hollywood, 1935

Plate 27, KATHARINE HEPBURN (b.1907)

A historic photograph that marks Horst's first use of the Rolleiflex camera. Its versatile square format and natural low angle allowed Horst to take outdoor snapshots that would have been impossible on the studio plate camera. Hepburn's hair is short for the film *Sylvia Scarlett*, in which she is disguised as a boy. In the 1930s, Hepburn was considered an unlikely candidate for Hollywood stardom, eschewing dresses for men's trousers. 'I never wear make-up and long ago I learned the joys of patched dungarees,' she told the writer James Watters, as Horst photographed her almost half a century later for a portrait that appeared in *Return Engagement*. She won her first Oscar in 1933 for her performance as Eva Lovelace in *Morning Glory*. She had been bankable since then, despite the trousers, the husky voice and the weeping eyes, a legacy of an infection picked up after a fall into the Grand Canal, Venice. Hepburn was a great friend of Huene, whom she knew in Hollywood through the film director George Cukor. *Vanity Fair* called her the stormy petrel of the RKO Studios. Perennially flying in the face of convention, the appeal of Katharine Hepburn was summed up by Lesley Cunliffe of *Vogue*: '[she] calls herself "a weatherbeaten old monument" which makes her sound like the Statue of Liberty. (Amazingly at eighty-three, she is nearly as old.) The Statue of Liberty might sound like Katharine Hepburn if she could change a tyre, do her own tree surgery and stand on her head for four minutes every day'. Horst let slip that, of all his sitters, he was always most nervous of her.
Taken: Hollywood, 1935

Plate 28, HELENA KUO (1913-99)

Kuo, a young Chinese author and lecturer, was praised by *Vogue* for 'dressing as well as she writes – with great distinction'. Born in Macao, Kuo was educated at a Portuguese convent and then at the University of Shanghai. In the 1930s she was a newspaper reporter, including the *Shanghai Daily News*. Escaping the Japanese invasion in 1937, she fled to Europe. For a short time she became a columnist for the *Daily Mail* in London (her first assignment was to write about a dog show) before emigrating again to the United States. She had written, as a long shot, a letter to Mrs Franklin D. Roosevelt, whose reply was encouraging and who helped her get to America. Apart from many articles for magazines and journals including *The China You Don't Know* for *Vogue* – a corrective to some misconceptions of her homeland – she wrote

four books. *Peach Path* was the first which, like *I've Come a Long Way*, was autobiographical. She was also special adviser to the production of the film *China* (1943) with Loretta Young and Alan Ladd. Once she handed a copy of *Vogue* to friends in Shanghai: 'Are Western people all that hungry?' asked one friend, looking at the stern-faced models, 'they look as if they haven't had anything to eat or any pleasure for weeks'.
Taken: New York, 1942
Published: American *Vogue*, 1 September 1942, pp.82-3

Plate 29, LUCHINO VISCONTI (COUNT VISCONTI DI MODRONE; 1906-76)

This informal portrait was taken in Hammamet at Huene and Horst's house. In 1935 Visconti was, as Valentine Lawford writes, 'to all appearances no more than a handsome representative of the rich and aristocratic Italian world into which he had been born'. Less kindly, he was an opera-loving dilettante, who carried pocket editions of Proust, Gide and Thomas Mann. Horst and Visconti had a torrid emotional entanglement that changed in time to a warm and lasting friendship. But it would always be fraught; in Hammamet Visconti irritated his friend by insisting Horst snap to attention when the Italian Fascist anthem blared from the radio, announcing an Italian victory in the Italo-Abyssinian war. A year after this picture was taken, Visconti became an apprentice to Jean Renoir and in 1942 directed his first film, *Ossessione*. From then until his death in 1975, he directed stage plays and opera, was a successful librettist, produced ballets and was an accomplished set designer. But it is for his films, classics of European cinema, that he will be remembered: *Rocco and His Brothers* (1960), *The Leopard* (1963), *Death in Venice* (1971) and his controversial study of Nazism, *The Damned* (of which Horst refused the première invitation). Horst was aware of the dichotomy at the heart of Visconti: a love of luxury and the grand gesture combined with genuine communist ideals and a profound sympathy with the underprivileged. In 1953 Horst recalled that 'he had many servants and they wore grey jackets with silver buttons. One of them was a very beautiful boy whose head had been shaved on Visconti's orders. He said the boy was too pretty and it wasn't good for him.'
Taken: Hammamet, Tunisia, 1935

Plates 30 AND 31, HELEN BENNETT

An early example of a beauty photograph by Horst. It shows a little of the playful *trompe l'œil* and surrealism that would characterize his more well-known examples: of 'Electric Beauty', or 'Waxed Beauty' for which Blanche Grady was the model. It also shows the direct influence of Huene, whose appropriation of ancient classical motifs was already apparent in his cool and elegant *Vogue* fashion photographs. Horst and Huene travelled together many times to Greece in the 1930s and studied ancient marbles, which they also inspected in Paris and at the British Museum in London. As he told British *Vogue* half a century later: 'I tried to learn from the marvellous old Greek statues, from the shapes and proportions – even the poses – of the bodies in Greek art … I stood in front of the

Acropolis and cried like a baby. It's funny those things ... but then the Surrealists came in and the whole thing loosened up.' Helen Bennett's head of curls is almost disembodied and with further cropping might have been completely so, for this appears to be an unpublished print. Whatever the intention, a pedestrian assignment (most likely to illustrate a hair style of the moment) is enlivened by the last vestiges of neo-Classicism and the first stirrings of Surrealism. In the special 'Photography' issue of American *Vogue*, June 1941, Helen Bennett was one of the eight most famous models to be profiled. The magazine revealed her height as 5' 7", her eyes as brown and hair 'ice-blond' confiding further that 'she knits beautifully' and had appeared in several Broadway shows.
Taken: 1936

Plate 32, GABRIELLE (COCO) CHANEL (1883-1971)

Horst and the great French couturière were lifelong friends – despite Horst being close to her hated rival Elsa Schiaparelli. This is his account of the sitting as told to Valentine Lawford: '... we arranged a session at the *Vogue* studio – a few wooden sculptures for the background, and I found the couch. She arrived with her assistant who was carrying her bags and gold jewellery ... This time she wasn't preoccupied with the photograph [Horst had photographed her before unsuccessfully]; she was thinking of a love affair with Paul Iribe that was ending. You can see that she's not paying attention to anything here – she's dreaming and thinking. She loved these pictures and ordered hundreds....' Chanel became one of the most famous names in twentieth-century fashion because she believed simply that what she would like to wear would appeal to women everywhere too. Thus she imposed her own style on the century: short hair, fake jewellery, an occasional sun-tan, mannish, comfortable clothes, a little make-up and the perfume Chanel No.5. In her long life she knew everyone worth knowing, from the Duke of Westminster to Diaghilev. When Horst refused payment for this sitting, she invited him to her home and took him on a tour of her magnificent furniture, much of it in store. Anything he chanced to admire was delivered to him the next morning.
Taken: Paris, 1937
Published: American *Vogue*, 1 December1937, p.86 (variant pose)

Plate 33, DUCHESS OF WINDSOR (1896-1986)

The most talked- and written-about woman of her generation, the chic American-born divorcée Mrs Wallis Simpson was seldom out of the pages of American *Vogue*. As her affair with the heir to the British throne escalated, British *Vogue* decreased its coverage of her dresses, menu lists, interior decoration tips and other random thoughts. ('The secret of running an attractive house is the personal touch ... In wartime one has to make just whirlwind tours every morning ...') The culmination of the Abdication Crisis occurred shortly before Christmas in 1936, when the heir became Edward VIII, King of England, and then renounced the throne to marry the woman he loved. The former king was given the title of Duke of Windsor, and he and

his future wife left for France. The subsequent aimless lifestyle of the exiled Duke and Duchess enthralled readers in Europe and America. To many, their relationship was perplexing and, in an article for *Vogue*, Valentine Lawford addressed it, asking the question rarely put in print: 'How many other women, one wonders, could have filled the void where a Kingdom was ...?' Of this sitting of the Duchess, taken in the Hotel Meurice just after her marriage, Horst recalled that 'on the mantle were just two photographs – Queen Mary and the Duke and Duchess with Hitler'. The picture appeared in *Vogue* with several snapshots of Horst taken by Roger Schall from behind arranging the set and then taking the finished composition.
Taken: Hotel Meurice, Paris, 1937
Published: American *Vogue*, 15 December 1937, pp.44-5

Plate 34, OLIVIA DE HAVILLAND (b.1916)

Horst photographed de Havilland in the 1930s and again for his book *Return Engagement* (1984). One of the great Hollywood actresses of the last century, she now lives in Paris, having moved there in 1955 to be with her second husband, Pierre Galante, the editor of *Paris-Match*. Her career began in swashbuckling epics, often opposite Errol Flynn, such as *Captain Blood* (1935) and *The Adventures of Robin Hood* (1938). The year after she played Maid Marian, she played Melanie Wilkes in *Gone with the Wind* (1939). *As Vanity Fair* noted recently, 'she has outlived all the film's leading actors by more than thirty years'. Quite apart from her legendary falling-out with her sister, Joan Fontaine, Olivia de Havilland is known for her test case against Warner Brothers, alleging that the studio was not giving her roles worthy of her talents. She would in time receive five Oscar nominations, winning two for *To Each His Own* (1946) and *The Heiress* (1949). Suspended for six months and out of work for two years, she won and obtained the landmark ruling still known as the 'De Havilland Decision', which limited forever the hold that studios could have over its contract players. This portrait of the young Miss de Havilland reveals a favourite Horst device, that of a portrait within a portrait frame, not true *trompe l'œil* but an approximation. In the following year, Horst arranged the couturière Elsa Schiaparelli in a similar pose, but in a far less baroque setting.
Taken: New York, 1936
Published: American *Vogue*, January 1937, p.54

Plate 35, DEANNA DURBIN (b.1921)

Although her career lasted barely a decade, no other actress trilled so sweetly in the 1930s and 1940s as Canadian-born Deanna Durbin. As Edna Mae Durbin (her real name) she starred with Judy Garland in *Every Sunday* and for her next film, *Three Smart Girls* (1936), she became 'Deanna' and an overnight success. After her film *Mad About Music* (1938), her hands were immortalized in wet cement outside Grauman's Chinese Theater. Along with fellow teenage phenomenon Mickey Rooney, she was awarded a special Oscar for 'a significant contribution in bringing to the screen the spirit and personification of youth'. After a string of hits, and the release of *For the Love of Mary* in 1948, she retired at the age of

twenty-seven to live outside Paris with her family, amid rumours of excessive weight gain. These stories apparently persisted and in 1980 she sent *Life* magazine a recent photograph of herself, saying 'I can still pass under the Arc de Triomphe without holding my breath'. The insouciant, smiling teenager in Horst's photograph belies the brief money-spinning industry her sweetness and singing created. The success of her second and third films – *Three Smart Girls* and *One Hundred Men and a Girl* – are frequently credited with rescuing Universal Studios from the brink of bankruptcy.
Published: American *Vogue*, 1 May 1938

Plate 36, MARGARET RAWLINGS (1906-96)

As a stage actress, Margaret Rawlings enjoyed a glorious career as a tragedienne and interpreter of Shavian comedies. She was 'magnetic', as one obituarist put it, 'rather than beautiful'. As a film actress, the parts offered her were frequently undemanding and occasionally beneath her. She first came to public attention in 1931 as Salome. Her 'Dance of the Seven Veils' was *risqué* enough to cause swooning among the audience. Horst photographed her in New York, where she was appearing in a play about Charles Parnell. In 1942 she married her second husband, Sir Robert Barlow, and retired for a while from the stage. She returned in *The White Devil* opposite her protégé Robert Helpmann and triumphed as Lady Macbeth opposite Alec Clunes. Appearing on stage in Sir Donald Wolfit's *Tamburlaine*, as the imprisoned Zabrina, she is alleged to have told Wolfit, a notorious fidgeter, that 'If you do that again, I'll rattle my chains through your next speech'. (She had no further trouble.) She was not beyond such scene-stealing herself. As Charmian in *Antony and Cleopatra* she continually upstaged the Russian actress Eugénie Leontovich's Cleopatra, whose performance was dreadful, leaving no one in any doubt as to who should have played the Queen of Egypt and who her handmaidens. In 1963 she retired again, but in 1978 returned to the West End to tremendous acclaim as Empress Eugénie in a dramatized monologue. Her film appearances were minor (mostly British B-movies and 'Hammer' horror films), though she was notable in *Roman Holiday* (1953), as Countess Vereberg, lady-in-waiting to Audrey Hepburn's Princess Ann.
Taken: As Katie O'Shea in *Parnell*, New York, 1935
Published: American *Vogue*, 15 January 1936, p.56

Plate 37, GINGER ROGERS (1911-95)

Fred Astaire's regular dancing partner, his sister Adèle, gave it all up in 1932 to marry Charles Cavendish, younger brother of the Duke of Devonshire. Into her shoes came Ginger Rogers, a Charleston contest-winning hoofer from Missouri. She had achieved fame by this time, chiefly as a nineteen-year-old ingénue in *Girl Crazy* opposite Alan Kearns. The elegance and grace she displayed in all her films, including the Astaire-Rogers collaborations, *Flying Down to Rio* (1933), *Top Hat* (1935), *The Gay Divorcee* (1934) and all the others, belied the hard work it took getting there, away from Independence, Missouri, and a father who, after a terrifying divorce, kidnapped her twice. And when the days with Astaire were over, she found herself the

bigger star. By 1945 she was the world's highest-paid movie actress and later became a musical comedy star on Broadway and in London with *Hello Dolly!* (1965) and *Mame* (1969). Her film career effectively ended in 1957 with *Oh, Men! Oh, Women!* Her work-ethic made her a popular nightclub entertainer and a television regular long after she could have gracefully retired and she had married and lost five husbands along the way. Of this session with Rogers, Horst wrote that at first he failed to recognize her because 'she was wearing a black hat dripping with grapes, cherries, leaves and flowers'.
Taken: New York, 1936
Published: American *Vogue*, 1 November 1936, pp.62-3

Plate 38, EVE CURIE (b.1904)

The daughter of the Nobel Prize-winning French chemists Pierre and Marie Curie, the isolaters of radium, Eve Curie distinguished herself as a pianist, music critic, lecturer and author. Her 1937 biography of her mother, *Marie Curie*, was translated into 32 languages. In 1940 she left Paris for London and in 1942 worked as a war correspondent in Libya, Russia, Burma and China. From 1942 to 1943 she served as a Lieutenant in the Women's Auxiliary Forces in the Free French Army. Horst shows her at the piano at her home in Paris where he attended one of her concerts. This study was part of a photo-essay on her life celebrating the success of the biography and was accompanied by text by Andre Maurois.
Published: American *Vogue*, 15 April 1938, p.74

Plate 39, EVE CURIE (b.1904)

This fashion study of Eve Curie posing in a dress by Schiaparelli, a black felt hat by Talbot and long black antelope gloves was one of a number taken by Horst and had appeared in *Vogue* in 1937. After the war, she was co-publisher of *Paris-Presse*, an evening newspaper in Paris (1944-9), and, together with her husband Henri Labouisse (d.1987), Curie was active in UNICEF and acted as Special Adviser to the Secretary-General of NATO in Paris from 1952 to 1954.
Published: French *Vogue*, 15 December 1937

Plate 40, BETTE DAVIS (1908-89)

Horst first photographed Davis in 1932 just before her seventh film, *The Man Who Played God*, was released for which she modelled a Bergdorf Goodman dress. Despite Horst's reservations ('I was not elated by it'), *Vanity Fair* ran the photograph. 'Probably', he recalled, 'because she was about to begin filming *Of Human Bondage*, opposite the great star Leslie Howard'. Later when I saw the film, I realised that at the sitting I had not understood her. In *Of Human Bondage*, she surprised everybody instantly with that great, pounding talent for which she is still justly famous.' When James Watters and Horst went to photograph her years later for *Return Engagement* (1984), they found her as provocative and funny despite having undergone a mastectomy and having suffered a stroke. Ronald Reagan, she thought, was 'a lousy little actor'. When Horst asked her to smile, she replied, 'A smile? That's not my natural tendency. I am an unsmiling woman ...' 'My mother', she

continued, 'was a photographer you know, and she was a great retoucher. I hope you are.' Horst then asked her if the light was too bright or too hot. 'I like 'em hot,' she drawled.
Taken: New York, 1939; Dress by Nettie Rosenstein
Published: American *Vogue*, 1 January 1941, p.36

Plate 41, JOAN CRAWFORD (1904-77)
A former waitress turned chorus girl, Lucille Le Sueur from San Antonio, Texas, made her debut as Joan Crawford in 1926, and by 1929 was a star. Her appeal was enduring, nearly eight years after this photograph was taken she received an Oscar for *Mildred Pierce* (1945). And decades after that, scored a huge hit opposite Bette Davis in Robert Aldrich's *guignol* masterpiece *Whatever Happened to Baby Jane?* (1962). Horst found her self-projection frustrating: 'She came in with an enormous fur coat and an enormous hat – she wanted to out do everybody ... You can't do anything with this type of girl – no contact whatsoever. The face – very strong – it's all make-up, a mask not a face ... she wanted me to imitate von Sternberg's lighting of Dietrich. At the time the lighting was very fashionable accentuating the arched eyebrows, the half-closed eyes, the cheeks pulled in, the hard mouth.'
Taken: New York, 1938
Published: American *Vogue*, 1 February 1938, p.103; British *Vogue*, 8 February 1939, p.46

Plate 42, ETHEL WATERS (1896-1977)
A soulful interpreter of the blues, Ethel Waters made popular, among others, the songs *Stormy Weather* and *Dinah*. She appeared in concert at Carnegie Hall, a year or two before her transition to straight plays on Broadway. Horst photographed her on her first appearance there as Hagar in the hit play *Mamba's Daughters*. She made many stage and film appearances including in *Blackbirds* (1930), *Rhapsody in Black* in the following year and later appeared as Petunia Jackson in *Cabin in the Sky* (1940) and Bernice in *The Member of the Wedding* (1950). In *Salute to the Thirties*, which featured this portrait, Valentine Lawford called her voice 'warm, strong, unforgettable'.
Taken: 1939
Published: American *Vogue*, 15 February 1939, p.61

Plate 43, EMLYN WILLIAMS (1905-87)
The playwright (George) Emlyn Williams appears here in *Night Must Fall*, a psychological thriller which he also wrote. The play proved to be a phenomenon, playing in London for over 435 performances and its success transferred to New York, where Horst photographed him. He is best known to modern audiences for a subsequent play and film, *The Corn is Green*, which he wrote, earning him the New York Drama Critics Circle Award of 1941. He was equally successful as an actor in other dramatists' works and as an inventive stage director. He achieved further success in a one-man performance as Charles Dickens reading excerpts of the Victorian writer's work. Inevitably for a Flintshire-born Welshman, he gave virtuoso performances and readings as Dylan Thomas. However, it did not meet with the same success. He was particularly proud

that his first play, *Full Moon*, playing in repertory at the Oxford Playhouse, produced a running-order that season which ran: 'Chekhov, Shaw, Barrie, Emlyn Williams, Strindberg'.
Taken: In *Night Must Fall*, New York,1935

Plate 44, BARBARA HUTTON, COUNTESS HAUGWITZ-REVENTLOW (1912-79)
By the time she sat for Horst, Barbara Hutton, the famous Woolworth heiress, had become by marriage the Countess Curt von Haugwitz-Reventlow. Her first husband had been Prince Alexis Mdivani. Her other husbands were Cary Grant, Prince Igor Troubetzkoy, the polo-playing lothario Porfirio Rubirosa, Baron Gottfried von Cramm and Prince Doan Vinh Na Chanpacak. Hutton is wearing a white satin dress embroidered with silver leaves designed by Chanel.
Taken: New York, 1939
Published: American *Vogue*, 1 March 1940, p.74; British *Vogue*, May 1940, p.24

Plate 45, SYLVIA, LADY ASHLEY, MRS DOUGLAS FAIRBANKS SNR (1904-77)
Born to humble origins Sylvia Hawkes rose to fame on the international stage as a leader of style and fashion through an early theatrical career and five marriages. As an ex-Gaiety girl, she appeared in the 1925 *Midnight Follies* where she caught the eye of Lord Ashley, son and heir of the Earl of Shaftesbury. They married in 1927 despite parental opposition on his side. Regularly featured in *Vogue* as a fashion leader in the late 1920s, the marriage to Lord Ashley ended in divorce proceedings in 1934. Hollywood's leading action hero, Douglas Fairbanks Snr, and her second husband-to-be, was cited as co-respondent. This marriage in 1936 lasted until his death in 1939. In 1941 she rejoined the British aristocracy by marrying Lord Stanley of Alderley. A two-year marriage to Clark Gable in 1949 was followed by a final marriage to Prince Dimitri Djardjadze. This portrait in *Vogue* shows her in silver sequins and pale blue chiffon and was one of four captioned 'They all like long sleeves'.
Taken: 1938
Published: American *Vogue*, 1 January 1939, p.67

Plate 46, LUD
The model Lud was a favourite of Horst and of Schiaparelli. In this, one of Horst's best-known fashion photographs, she wears a dress by Alix (later known as Madame Grès), whose hallmark was draping material in a 'classical' style, which appealed to Horst and Huene's love of the ancient civilizations. It is, as Horst admitted, heavily influenced by Steichen's portrait of Isadora Duncan at the Parthenon. Horst said of Lud: 'I spotted her when she was working as a messenger. She was delivering a package at the *Vogue* studio and I immediately wanted to use her as a model ... She revolutionized the look of the model. She was not at all remote or cold, not at all like a sleepwalker; she was sensual and catlike. When I met her she was poor, and lived with her brother on a boat in the Seine. No amount of money could get her to pose in a dress she did not like. She had an aversion to jewels ... She fell in love with a lion tamer and

married him and the two of them travelled with the circus.'
Taken: In a dress by Alix, *Vogue* Studio, Paris, 1938
Published: French *Vogue*, April 1938, p.55; American *Vogue*, 1938, p.75

Plate 47, JESSICA TANDY (1907-94)
One of the most versatile stage actresses of her time, British-born Jessica Tandy made America her home from the late 1930s. Her early career in England spawned successes such as *Autumn Crocus* (1934) and *Mädchen in Uniform* (1932). By 1947 such was her appeal on the American stage that she was chosen to create the role of Blanche du Bois in Tennessee Williams' *A Streetcar Named Desire* opposite Marlon Brando. Married twice, firstly in 1932 to British lantern-jawed character actor Jack Hawkins, and then ten years later she settled in California with actor Hume Cronyn, with whom she occasionally acted. At the time of this sitting she was appearing as the rebellious little Irish girl in *The White Steed*. Later in her career, she appeared in Albee's *All Over* in New York (1971), and she won an Oscar for her performance in Bruce Beresford's *Driving Miss Daisy* (1989).
Taken: New York, 1938
Published: American *Vogue*, 15 February 1939, p.65 (variant pose)

Plate 48, GARY COOPER (1901-61) AND HIS WIFE 'ROCKY' (VERONICA BALFE; 1914-2000)
Arriving in Los Angeles with $200, Gary Cooper tried his hand as a photographer's assistant, which he found as unsatisfying as it was unprofitable. Gary Cooper's career started as a film extra in Westerns on $5 a day in 1925 before he got his big break as second lead in a film starring Ronald Colman and Vilma Banky, *The Winning of Barbara Worth* (1926). His hit films of the 1930s included *Lives of a Bengal Lancer* (1935) and *Mr Deeds Goes to Town* (1936) which demonstrated his skills, in the first, as action hero and in the second as adept player of light social comedy. He won Oscars for *Sergeant York* (1941) and *High Noon* (1952), the film that best personified his laconic monosyllabic style that made him a quintessential Western star. Cooper was publicized for his romantic escapades with, among others, Clara Bow and Lupe Velez before he settled down to marriage with actress, sports champion and socialite Veronica Balfe, nicknamed 'Rocky'. Balfe appeared in a few films in the 1930s as Sandra Shaw in small parts, most notably as the woman dropped by the giant ape in *King Kong* (1933). This sombre brooding study was not published. An alternative smiling pose in different outfits was run in *Vogue* as a pair to another film couple photographed by Toni Frissell, the Fred Astaires.
Published: French *Vogue*, November 1938, p.64; American *Vogue*, 15 January 1939, p.68 (alternative sitting)

Plate 49, JANET GAYNOR (1906-84) and ADRIAN (1903-59)
Unusually for Hollywood, theirs was a marriage that lasted twenty years broken only by Adrian's death in 1959. During the 1930s Janet Gaynor was as big a box-office draw as Garbo,

especially after *A Star is Born* (1937), with Adolphe Menjou and Fredric March. She married the Hollywood dress designer, known simply as 'Adrian', in 1939 and all but disappeared from the screen. Her place in cinematic history was assured by the award to her of the first ever Oscar (in 1929 for *Seventh Heaven*). After designing productions for Rudolph Valentino and Cecil B. De Mille, Adrian became Chief Costume Designer for MGM, designing for Garbo, Norma Shearer, Jean Harlow and Joan Crawford (most memorably her evening gown in *Grand Hotel*). His 'coat-hanger look' of padded shoulders and a slim skirt returned as the epitome of 1980s 'power-dressing'. The fashion historian Colin McDowell puts a strong case for him being 'the most influential designer of his time' in light of the field in which he operated and the size of his audience. In 1942 he opened his own fashion house in Beverly Hills and another in New York in 1948. The fashion designer was also a painter *manqué* and showed his work, influenced by travels to exotic places, with some success.
Taken: 1940

Plate 50, INGRID BERGMAN (1915-82) and BURGESS MEREDITH (1908-97)
Bergman had been a star in Sweden since the age of seventeen. Seven years later in 1939 she made her first Hollywood film, *Intermezzo*, with Leslie Howard. Horst met her for the first time a year after that and photographed her with Burgess Meredith – they were appearing together in *Liliom*, her first Broadway role. Meredith had a long successful film and stage career, both as an actor and director. His third wife was the actress Paulette Goddard. As a stage actress, Bergman appeared in *Anna Christie* and *Joan of Lorraine*. Her Hollywood films are acknowledged classics: *Casablanca* (1942), *For Whom the Bell Tolls* (1943), *Notorious* (1946), and she won Oscars for *Gaslight* (1944) and *Anastasia* (1956). Bergman was deemed unemployable in America after her desertion of her husband and daughter for an affair with the Italian director Roberto Rossellini whilst making *Stromboli* (1949). It was not until the end of this second marriage and the making, in London, of *Anastasia* that her career was resurrected.
Taken: New York, 1940
Published: American *Vogue*, 1 May 1940, p.66

Plate 51, VERONICA LAKE (1919-75)
Born Constance Ockleman, she entered films in 1939 as Constance Keane, before changing her name in 1941, the year of this photograph, to Veronica Lake to become one of Hollywood's most popular wartime actresses. Veronica Lake captivated audiences. By the time the war was over her brief career was on the wane. Her trademark was her long, luxuriant hair, famously permed into a 'peek-a-boo' style. This occurred apparently by chance when, at a publicity photo shoot, a lock of her hair fell down over one eye. Straightaway she was put under contract to Paramount and cast alongside William Holden and Ray Milland in *I Wanted Wings* (1941), her big break. The comedy *Sullivan's Travels* (1941) followed. She partnered Alan Ladd in the *film noir* classics *The Glass Key*

(1942), *This Gun for Hire* (1942) and later *The Blue Dahlia* (1946). Unfortunately for her career, the State Department asked the studio to compel her to pull back her hair from her face, alarmed that imitation 'Veronica Lake' hair styles were leading to accidents on factory floors as hair tangled with machinery. And when her hair went back, the film roles decreased. She also had an alcohol dependency which made her, by many accounts, 'difficult to work with'. By the late 1960s, she had slipped completely from view and was found working as a barmaid in New York City. Horst's portrait places her in a moody, *noir*-ish milieu complete with a shadowy male figure in the foreground, as in the style of the best of her films. As the portrait bears witness, the State Department's message appears to have hit home with Paramount and Lake.
Taken: New York, 1941

Plate 52, MERLE OBERON, LADY KORDA (1911-79)
In 1942 Merle Oberon's husband, the film-maker Alexander Korda, was knighted and so as Lady Korda she embarked on her own war effort. *Vogue* reported on her hard work and its successes. In New York, just back from a five-week tour of American Expeditionary Force camps in England and Ireland in the company of Al Jolson, Patricia Morison and Frank McHugh, she was en route for Hollywood. This portrait was part of 'Bundles for Britain', a wartime campaign to aid Britain in its darkest hour. Horst first photographed Merle Oberon in London in the early 1930s, where she was making Korda's *The Private Life of Don Juan* with Douglas Fairbanks Snr.
Taken: New York, 1942
Published: American *Vogue*, 15 November 1942, p.30

Plate 53, MYRNA LOY (1905-93)
One of America's best-loved actresses, Myrna Loy, the daughter of a Montana cattle rancher, struggled for years as the exotic interest in *The Thief of Baghdad* (1924), *Ben Hur* (1925) and *The Mask of Fu Man Chu* (1932). As James Watters puts it in the book *Return Engagement*: 'In over 100 movies nothing threw her – Creoles, Chinese dolls, gypsy wildcats and black-faced waitresses as well as murderesses, perfect wives and alcoholic mothers.' Her sixty-fourth movie in 1934 was her true breakthrough, as the first of six films in *The Thin Man* series opposite the suave William Powell. Her own favourite role was in *The Best Years of Our Lives* (1946), as Fredric March's wife. The same year she showed the public another side, by appearing as a member of the audience at a Security Council debate of the fledgling United Nations. She later became an active member of UNESCO. Horst's photograph was taken as part of 'Bundles for Britain'. Loy's duty here was to advertise gloves for sale.
Taken: New York, 1942
Published: American *Vogue*, 15 November 1942, p.31

Plate 54, MARLENE DIETRICH (1901-92)
Dietrich's Hollywood film career was launched by the impact she made in the Josef von Sternberg-directed film *The Blue Angel* (1930). Sent from Hollywood to make the film in Berlin, he spotted Dietrich on the Berlin stage. Dietrich followed von

Sternberg back to Hollywood, where his directorial skills and inspired lighting combined with Dietrich's acting skills and star presence and they began to create the Dietrich legend in the six films they worked on. These included *Morocco* (1930), *Dishonored* (1931), *Shanghai Express* (1932), *The Scarlet Empress* (1934) and *The Devil is a Woman* (1935). Horst had known Dietrich before this photograph was taken. On one occasion during the war, when both had elected to serve with the Allies, they dined together in New York in their American forces uniforms. Naturally they both spoke German to each other, which caused a minor diplomatic incident. Horst was the first to hear the songs she had recorded to broadcast to the German troops on the Western Front to persuade then to lay down their arms.
Taken: New York, 1942
Published: American *Vogue*, 1 July 1942, p.34 (variant pose)

Plate 55, MARLENE DIETRICH (1901-92)
Horst claimed that Hollywood movie stars assumed the places left vacant by vanishing European royalty, and his experience of French society in the inter-war years convinced him that even the most formidable of Parisian dowagers would 'go anywhere for a sandwich' whenever celebrity of whatever kind was in town. The fiercely intellectual Vicomtesse de Noailles was known to camp out in the Hotel Trianon-Palace in Versailles on the off-chance that she might catch a glimpse of Marlene Dietrich. Of this sitting, Horst recalled that 'she came in wearing this terrible hat and in that voice said "Remember the von Sternberg lighting". The Sternberg lighting had the shadow under the nose and she would pull in her cheeks, so there would be a deep shadow there. I moved the light down slightly below her face and made the light softer and all the wrinkles disappeared.' When he was making *Kismet* (1944), Horst received a telegram asking him to explain how he had lit this portrait. The chair over which Dietrich leans has a needlepoint design made by Eleonora von Mendelssohn based on one of Horst's still-life compositions.
Taken: New York, 1942
Published: American *Vogue*, 1 July 1942, p.35

Plate 56, SALVADOR DALÍ (1904-89)
Dalí was another sitter known to Horst before being photographed by him. Dalí and his waxed moustaches were seldom out of the headlines and he remained active as a painter, illustrator, set designer, author and iconoclast and famous just for being Salvador Dalí. He collaborated with Coco Chanel to produce costumes for Massine's ballet *Bacchanale*. The choreographer found them impractical and they were never used, but *Vogue* ran the picture anyway. The eve of war marked the first time that Horst worked with Dalí. '[He] had just broken with Surrealism,' recalled Horst and Dalí left Paris for New York in 1940 and rarely went back. Horst had an ambivalent relationship with the Surrealists left behind because they were so disapproving of Jean Cocteau, one of Horst's closest friends. Later, after the war was over, Dalí, now based in the St Regis Hotel, designed surrealist settings for Horst's fashion pictures. In post-war New York, he was still interested enough in fashion to create some surrealist window displays for

the department store Bonwit Teller which were, according to Horst, 'sensational'. Once, while re-arranging a part of the display, in a late burst of involuntary avant-gardism, he tumbled through a plate glass window onto Fifth Avenue but somehow managed to remain standing upright. Horst and Dalí remained friends until the painter's death.
Taken: New York, 1943

Plate 57, LEONOR FINI (1908-96)

Born in Argentina, Fini's heritage was Slavic, Venetian, German, Spanish and Neapolitan. A painter and illustrator, she is best known today for her decadent, semi-surrealistic works of the 1930s in which sex and death played key roles. She exhibited in Paris in 1935 and three years later held her first show in New York, introduced by Giorgio di Chirico. In her idiosyncratic manner, she illustrated the sonnets of Shakespeare and the work of the Marquis de Sade, as well as creating memorable sets for the ballet and stage. *Vogue* found much to admire in her 'vicious arabesques' and noted that she had just completed a book of pornographic drawings 'which should join the classics in the field'. In 1949 Les Ballets de Paris presented *Le Rêve de Leonor Fini* with music by Benjamin Britten. This portrait, revealing her flamboyant character, was taken in her Paris home (she also lived in Rome). 'Leonor Fini was independent and determined', recalled Horst, 'and didn't want to belong to any set like Cocteau's or Janet Flanner's or Gertrude Stein's – not like Man Ray, who ran around trying to know everyone.'
Taken: Paris, 1946

Plate 58, DUCHESS OF WINDSOR (1896-1986)

Taken: Waldorf Astoria Hotel, New York, 1943

Plate 59, DUCHESS OF WINDSOR (1896-1986)

Horst photographed the Duchess of Windsor many times, the Duke only once at their house in the Bois de Boulogne. The Duke insisted on being given time to brush his hair and on speaking to Horst in German. Frequently he photographed the Duchess in hotel suites across the world, including the Hotel Meurice in Paris and the Waldorf Astoria in New York. In both these portraits, the Duchess wears clothes designed by the American Mainbocher, her favourite couturier and the main contributor to her legendary wardrobe. It was Mainbocher who designed her dress and trousseau for her wedding in 1937 at the Château de Candé; the Duchess appearing in 'Wallis' blue, a particular shade of sapphire. 'Her skill', reported *Vogue*, 'is with the modern, the precise and the understated.' A seated version of this portrait became one of the Duke's favourites. Horst recalled that 'it was difficult to find a prop for her. It couldn't be overpowering (Her taste was influenced by Elsie Mendl's). I put the parquet flooring down for the photograph.'
Taken: In a Mainbocher dress, New York, 1947
Published: American *Vogue* (variant seated pose published in black-and-white 15 May 1947, p.89)

Plate 60, ARTURO TOSCANINI (1867-1957)

In a life that was as long as it was tempestuous, Toscanini was

an uncompromising and difficult genius; one who suffered 'a kind of physical agony', according to *Vogue*, 'if a member of his orchestra was to make a mistake'. Toscanini conducted the world première of Puccini's *La Bohème* in 1896, prompting the composer to remark in awe that the maestro had managed to bring to the music what he had imagined in his head but had failed adequately to write down. A decade before that, he had played cello in the first performance of Verdi's *Otello*, later conducting the first of *Pagliacci*. For the first time in Italy, he conducted Wagner's *Götterdämmerung*, *Die Meistersinger* and *Siegfried*. For thirty-three years he based himself in the United States (with time off to oversee La Scala, Milan, and the Bayreuth and Salzburg festivals). With the Metropolitan Opera for seven years and the New York Philharmonic for ten, he remained with the NBC Symphony Orchestra (specially created for him) for seventeen years. Aged eighty-eight, he had his final concert in 1954. When he came to the three chords that end the overture to *Die Meistersinger*, he indicated the first two with his baton and on the third dropped it, bowed once and walked off to his dressing room to weep. After a standing ovation, he was only able to leave the auditorium by the main door, the audience had gone to the stage door to acclaim him further. This was the first colour photograph he had ever sat for but, according to Horst, he didn't so much sit, but fidget and act suspiciously of the lens as if it was to do him an injustice.
Taken: New York, 1940
Published: American *Vogue*, 1 April 1940, p.58

Plate 61, ALICIA MARKOVA (b.1910)

A member of Sergei Diaghilev's Ballets Russes (1924-29), Markova returned to Britain to dance at Vic-Wells (later Sadlers Wells and Royal Ballet). Noted for her interpretations of *Giselle* in her collaboration with Anton Dolin and the creation of the Markova-Dolin Company in 1935 which toured internationally before becoming successively the London Festival Ballet (1949) and English National Ballet (1988). When Horst photographed her, Markova was prima ballerina of The Ballet Theatre, shortly to open in New York in two pieces: *Beloved* and Fokine's *Bluebeard*. This is a variant of a colour portrait of the British star taken for *Vogue*. And with such 'expressive flower hands', the magazine could not resist the opportunity for a beauty shot too. Her nails were painted in a new Revlon shade, 'Hothouse Rose'. Some time later for Horst's colleague John Rawlings at *Vogue* she divulged her 'Twelve Point Maquillage', some homespun beauty treatments (bathing her feet in lukewarm milk) and some dietary tips: 'I *adore* potatoes'.
Taken: New York, 1941
Published: American *Vogue*, 15 October 1941, p.51 (variant pose)

Plate 62, GENE TIERNEY (1920-91)

Born in Brooklyn and educated in Switzerland, Gene Tierney was, according to *Vogue*, 'one of the biggest stars in Hollywood. She speaks French fluently, loves parties and the smell of gasoline and paint'. She played the beautiful widow in *The Ghost and Mrs Muir* (1947). She was also an occasional model

for *Vogue*; unsurprisingly, considering the regular appearance of her own husband's creations in the fashion pages – he was the fashion designer Oleg Cassini. A Florentine count, he started his career designing costumes on the films of Gene Tierney, and served as dress-designer-in-residence to the White House during the era of Jacqueline Kennedy. Horst's portrait of Tierney with disembodied likenesses of the actress reflects the surrealist-inspired motifs that appear particularly in his beauty photographs of the period.
Taken: New York, 1941 (Portrait masks by Lillian Bettinger)
Published: American *Vogue*, 1 June 1940, p.68; British *Vogue*, August 1940, p.36

Plate 63, MURIEL MAXWELL
Another cover for American *Vogue* that found its way to the other international edition of the magazine in London. One of Horst's less abstruse compositions – a surrealist, eye-catching arrangement done of course with mirrors to ensure a multiple perspective. It also serves to enliven what appears to be a peculiar and unflattering choice of headwear. Muriel Maxwell was another of Horst's favourite models from the Powers agency, 'She was one of Mr Nast's favourite models. Like Helen Bennett, she was one of the first American girls to be sent to the Paris Collections. She was tall and like most of the girls, someone with good manners. Her father was a Rabbi.' Later she became a fashion editor at *Vogue* but appears to have had a luckless life after that. According to the designer Bill Blass, in interview with Michael Gross for his book *Model*: 'Muriel Maxwell, my God, she was on welfare before she died. Tragedy after tragedy ....'
Taken: New York, 1940
Published: American *Vogue*, 1 August 1940 (cover)

Plate 64, AMERICAN and BRITISH *VOGUE* COVERS (original tearsheets)
a. Bettina Bollegard, 1 November 1941
b. Muriel Maxwell, 1 August 1940
c. Helen Bennett, 15 May 1938
d. Helen Bennett, April 1940
e. Lisa Fonssagrives, 1 June 1940
f. Lisa Fonssagrives, 1 September 1940

Plate 65, HELEN HAYES (1900-93)
Despite enjoying a successful film career, winning two Oscars, for Best Actress for *The Sin of Madelon Claudet* in 1931 and, forty years later, Best Supporting Actress for *Airport* (1970), it is as a Broadway actress that Helen Hayes was best known, in her role in *Victoria Regina* (1935-8). In 1955 The Fulton Theater was renamed the Helen Hayes Theater to celebrate her Broadway Jubilee. Here, Horst photographs her in costume as Viola in *Twelfth Night*. A few years later he photographed her 16-year-old daughter Mary MacArthur (her father was the playwright Charles MacArthur), who followed in her footsteps. They acted together in J. M. Barrie's *Alice-Sit-by-the-Fire* (1946).
Taken: New York, 1940
Published: American *Vogue*, 1 December 1940, p.97 (variant pose)

Plate 66, PAULETTE GODDARD (1905-90)
Though she had acted for at least a decade, it was Charlie Chaplin's *Modern Times* in 1936 that secured Goddard's reputation as an actress of distinction. She also married Chaplin in the same year, and acted with him again in *The Great Dictator* (1940). Her subsequent husbands were Burgess Meredith and the German writer Erich Maria Remarque, famous for the best-selling anti-war novel *All Quiet on the Western Front*. Goddard and Remarque lived together in Switzerland until his death in 1970. Lawford remarks that, shortly before Remarque's death, Horst sat between 'the once-famous German novelist and the once-world-famous film star, and was unforgettably impressed by the number of middle-aged American tourists who couldn't resist the temptation to pay their respects before passing on'.
Taken: New York, 1941
Published: American *Vogue*, 15 January 1941, p.63 (variant pose)

Plate 67, LORETTA YOUNG (1913-2000)
With the fluffy look of a round-eyed kitten (as *Vogue* put it in 1932), Loretta Young's career in films started at the age of five. She was a screaming child on an operating table in a Fannie Ward vehicle of 1918. Born in Salt Lake City, she was one of four beautiful sisters (the other three were Polly Ann Young, Georgiana Montalban and Sally Blane). For most of her early career, she played docile, home-loving heroines but during the 1930s expanded her repertoire with *Midnight Mary* (1933) playing a murderess from the city slums. Her co-stars were the matinée idols of the golden age of Hollywood: Charles Boyer, Gary Cooper, Douglas Fairbanks Jnr, Ronald Colman, Clark Gable and Cary Grant. She was nicknamed the 'Iron Madonna' for her Catholic faith and her steely, determined professionalism, which led her to produce a long-running televison show, *Loretta Young*. Horst's portrait appeared in *Vogue* to celebrate her films *Bedtime Story* and *The Men in Her Life* (both 1941). She was a 'master of the philosophy of being a woman – she crowns her candid beauty with a huge hat of spun glass and lace'.
Taken: New York, 1941
Published: American *Vogue*, 15 June 1941, p.38

Plate 68, JANE FONDA (b.1937)
This intimate portrait of Jane Fonda predates her activism by a decade, and coincides with the start of her film career. When it was taken she was still a model, and this is her all-American appeal reclining during assignment at Horst's home in Oyster Bay. Throughout the 1950s, he carried out many advertising commissions when it started to be a serious business again after the war. Jane Fonda featured twice on the cover of *Vogue*. From an acting dynasty, she was in many Hollywood films before *Barbarella*, but it is Roger Vadim's sci-fi extravaganza of 1968 and the charming *Barefoot in the Park* from the year before that identify her closely with the 1960s and the first half of her career. Increasingly politicized by America's military involvement with Vietnam, she became 'Hanoi Jane', an

outspoken and articulate public figure. From then on she gave memorable 'serious' performances in films like *Klute* (1971), *Coming Home* (1978), *Comes A Horseman* (1978) and *On Golden Pond* (1981) with her father and screen veteran Henry Fonda. She announced her retirement from the screen in 1991.
Taken: Horst's House, Oyster Bay, Long Island, New York, 1959
Published: American *Vogue*, 1 September 1959, p.203

Plate 69, EDITH SITWELL (1887-1964)

Long regarded as a curiosity in Britain for her early poems, which taken at face value could be nonsensical, for her flair for attracting publicity for herself and her brothers, Sitwell was rapturously received in the United States. Horst photographed her in the *Vogue* studio, New York, during a recital tour. 'She is fantastic, definite, an eccentric,' pronounced *Vogue* in an unconscious parody of her own wordplay. Later she would go to Hollywood, where she was enchanted with Marilyn Monroe. She feuded famously with many sacred cows, including Noël Coward, who delighted her by walking out of the first performance of her long poem *Façade* (1922) with experimental lines such as 'Also the hairy sky that we/Take for a coverlet comfortably'. Accompanied by the music of William Walton, she recited through a megaphone. Horst's recollection of her: 'Edith Sitwell wore extravagant clothes and jewels; usually the clothes did not fit at all, they just hung ... She was very proud of her nose and said "Oh this is a Plantagenet nose" ... I wanted a very strong picture with a defined shape. I wanted to make the connection to Old England and literature.' Horst lunched with her at Oyster Bay and introduced her to Garbo, of whom she commented, 'A charming woman. Not at all like an actress.'
Taken: New York, 1948

Plate 70, LILY CUSHING, MRS WILLIAM T. EMMET

Lily Dulany Cushing was the daughter of the Boston-born portrait painter Howard Gardiner Cushing. She followed her father's profession and according to *Vogue*'s caption writer, 'has painted every day, all day, since childhood – through her debutante year and married life'. (Her husband was William T. Emmet, by whom she had two daughters.) One of her gouaches, *Street in Saugherties*, was in the Museum of Modern Art, New York. Another of her drawings was sold in the 1996 Jacqueline Kennedy sale for a five-figure sum.
Taken: In her studio, New York, 1942
Published: American *Vogue*, 15 February 1942, p.45

Plate 71, TALLULAH BANKHEAD (1903-68)

Bankhead posed regally for Horst in a costume designed by Aline Berstein, for her role as the Queen in Ronald Duncan's adaptation of Cocteau's romantic melodrama *The Eagle Has Two Heads* (from *La Mort Ecoute aux Portes*). The play had a long try-out tour before being premièred at New York's Plymouth Theatre on 19 March 1947 and is notable, apart from closing after only 29 performances, for having the young Marlon Brando in the original cast before Bankhead sacked him. He exploded to fame later that year as Stanley Kowalski

in Tennesse Williams' *A Streetcar Named Desire*. It was produced by John C. Wilson, who was Noël Coward's former manager and business partner, as well as being the husband of another of Huene and Horst's friends, Natasha Paley.
Taken: In *The Eagle Has Two Heads*, Plymouth Theater, New York, 1947

Plate 72, TALLULAH BANKHEAD (1903-68)

Her distinctive husky voice, her rapier wit, her flamboyant lifestyle and her off-stage activities have all tended to overshadow Tallulah Bankhead's accomplishments as a leading stage actress. After *Lady of the Camellias*,' *Vogue* was moved to compare her to Sarah Bernhardt and Eleanora Duse. Though her début was as a teenager in New York in 1918, it was on the London stage that the Alabama-born ingénue found her earliest success and she was, for a time, a committed Anglophile. Of her London days, *Vanity Fair* observed that she became almost instantly the giddiest kind of public idol. Her gowns, her gestures, her house in Mayfair have been of passionate interest.' The role of Miss Flood in *Reflected Glory* lured Bankhead back to the States in 1936 and was a hit. Even more successful was *The Little Foxes* (1939); photographed here in her role as Regina Giddens, and she was also notable in Noël Coward's *Private Lives*.
Taken: In *The Little Foxes* New York, 1939
Published: American *Vogue*, 1 August 1939, p.31

Plate 73, LISA FONSSAGRIVES (1911-92)

Lisa Fonssagrives was the most successful professional model of her time and in the days before models opened restaurants or studied acting, her face was one of America's most recognizable icons of contemporary beauty. She was Horst's favourite model a decade before she became Irving Penn's favourite, and whom she married in 1950. Horst and Fonssagrives started out together; Horst remembered her 'trembling with fear' but recognized her potential straightaway. 'On the day of my first test with Horst, I was terrified,' she recalled years later, 'I knew nothing about fashion and had never even looked at a fashion magazine. I had no idea what was expected of me. I didn't know what to do with my hands or how to pose. Horst was very kind to me but was nearly as inexperienced as I was.' As Horst simplified his approach to fashion photography, some of his best photographs taken were of Lisa and they rely, as her biographer Martin Harrison has suggested, 'on very little other than Horst's mastery of studio lighting and the graphic power of his compositions'.
Taken: New York, 1940; published American *Vogue*, November 1940, p.51

Plate 74, GLORIA VANDERBILT (b.1924)

As a child in the 1930s, Gloria Vanderbilt was at the centre of a notorious custody battle played out between her mother and her paternal grandmother. Horst included this pensive study in his book of photographs *Salute to the Thirties*, despite it being taken in the 1940s. This is in part due to her childhood always having been under public scrutiny and also because

Horst considered her 'one of the most attractive and original American women he has ever known'.
Taken: New York, 1941
Published: American *Vogue*, 15 January 1942, pp.48-9 (variant standing pose)

Plate 75, MILADA MLADOVA (b.1922)
'A young discovery' of the Monte Carlo Ballet, trumpeted *Vogue*. Horst photographed the Czech-born American at the age of seventeen after her first successful season for *Vogue*. She triumphed as a soloist in *The Seventh Symphony*. The feature was entitled 'Ballerinas in Bathing Suits' and the set of pictures was spread over several pages of the Christmas issue. It marks one of the earliest attempts by Horst to inject some indication of movement into his pictures. Though still static, the athletic figure of Mladova complements the swimwear as much as Horst's early fashion photographs of Lisa Fonssagrives. He always admired the fluid figures of dancers (Fonssagrives had also trained as a ballerina). Mladova liked one of the articles of swimwear *Vogue* provided: 'She decided it would be perfect for rehearsals', reported *Vogue*, 'and she ordered it on the spot'.
Taken: In Jantzen's 'Velva-Lur' suit from Harrods, New York, 1939
Published: American *Vogue*, 15 December 1938; British *Vogue*, 31 May 1939, p.62

Plate 76, CARMEN DELL'OREFICE (b.1931)
Carmen Dell'Orefice has been a model for nearly sixty years. Grown men squabble over her provenance: she was allegedly discovered on the top of a bus by Clifford Coffin, although Herman Landshoff's wife claims the honour too. Cecil Beaton insisted that he photographed her first, though it may well be Horst. But it was perhaps with Norman Parkinson that she did her most famous work and she moved him to hyperbole, 'She is the Empress answer to all those dressed-up teenager nymphets who find themselves zipped into Yves Saint-Laurent ballgowns by fashion editors who are in mourning for their own brief youths.' She affected Horst too: 'Although only a sixteen-year-old school girl, she possesses an inherent gracefulness rarely found except among primitive races. Her almond-shaped eyes are those of a Renaissance beauty, a soft revelation when looking up.' He goes on to tell us how she moves ('softly like an animal') and concludes that 'she has the two primary requisites of true elegance: the physical attributes of youth and the languour of the past. She is an American beauty of an antique other age.' Whatever the quality she had for Horst, Carmen still has it and continues to model on the catwalk and off. She was tactful enough to repay their adulation: 'I was very spoiled,' she has said of Horst, Beaton, Penn and the others. 'They showed me what manhood was about, really. I was madly in love.' She was photographed most recently for British *Vogue*'s Millennium issue by Nick Knight.
Taken: *Vogue* Studio, New York, 1947

Plate 77, LADY DIANA COOPER (1892-1986)
The daughter of the 8th Duke of Rutland, Lady Diana Cooper was one of the last century's great English beauties and appeared as the Madonna in Max Rheinhardt's *The Miracle* to international acclaim. This portrait of Diana Cooper was taken while she and her husband, Sir Alfred Duff Cooper, were on a visit to the United States just after the outbreak of war. A former First Lord of the Admiralty, Sir Alfred had resigned from the British Goverment as a protest against the Munich Pact of 1938, though Valentine Lawford suggests that, 'Lady Diana's ... beauty was perhaps even more famous than her husband's stand against the policy of appeasement'. This was the first time that American *Vogue* found such distinguished social and political Britons in its midst. Horst thought the sitting went remarkably well, considering that 'Condé Nast was proud and impressed, and Margaret Case [*Vogue*'s Society Editor] was in a state of excitement bordering on hysteria'. (And taking into account Duff Cooper's well-known hostility towards Horst's homeland.) 'Duff Cooper was genial and cooperative and Lady Diana treated me as a friend, not merely because she had a naturally free-and-easy manner, but more particularly, I felt, because she and I had close acquaintances in common.' Duff Cooper became Britain's first post-war ambassador to Paris and was later created Viscount Norwich. Lady Diana wrote three volumes of memoirs and in her long life was rarely out of the fashion, beauty and social pages of *Vogue*.
Taken: New York, 1940
Published: American *Vogue*, 1 March 1940, p.66; British *Vogue*, April 1940, pp.50-1 (from a sitting with her husband Alfred Duff Cooper)

Plate 78, MILLICENT ROGERS (1902-53)
An heiress to the Standard Oil fortune, Millicent Rogers was an extravagant and generous benefactress (she raised over a million dollars for aid to war-torn Europe and Asia). She was also a fashion icon of her day with an idiosyncratic style. She would finish off a couturier's ensemble with a cheap and shiny head-dress from Chinatown or ask leading designers such as Mainbocher to create dresses for her in the style of, say, the court of Louis-Philippe. In Austria, where she owned a house filled with Biedermeier furniture, she would go back a little to nature: after research trips to the folk museum at Innsbruck, she liked to have her village tailor make up dirndl skirts and aprons, Tyrolean hats and pretty scarves in local colours. These she might team with something from Schiaparelli. Across the world in Taos, New Mexico, she would do much the same, wandering around her magnificent adobe house in ethnic clothes and jewellery. So taken was she with the craftsmanship of local jewellery makers, that she became a gifted designer herself in turquoise and coral. Her legacy is the Millicent Rogers Memorial Museum near Taos, founded by her son, which houses her collections of costumes and jewellery. Schiaparelli mused in her autobiography that 'had she not been so terribly rich [Rogers] might, with her vast talent and unlimited generosity, have become a great artist'.
Taken: New York, December 1938
Published: American *Vogue*, 1 January 1939, p.38

Plate 79, RITA HAYWORTH (1918-87)

Hayworth was, according to *Life* magazine, 'The Love Goddess'. Of Spanish, Irish and American ancestry, she was born Margarita Carmen Cansino and from an early age, she joined her father's troupe of exotic exhibition dancers, specializing in ballroom techniques. Georgina Howell wrote in a *Vogue* profile: 'Rita Hayworth made the Hollywood legend come true, from the Obscure Beginning, the Change of Name to the Big Build-up and the Instant Box Office Success.' After a start in B-movies, she made it to main features, Hollywood stardom and popular adulation in Howard Hawks' *Only Angels Have Wings* (1939). She also starred memorably as Dora Sol, opposite Tyrone Power in *Blood and Sand* (1941). She is alleged to have got the part after the actress of choice, a blonde, refused to dye her hair red. Other successes were *Gilda* (1946), *Salome* (1953) and *You Were Never Lovelier* (1942). She married famously – Orson Welles and the Aly Khan – and had a daughter by each marriage. Her film *Cover Girl* (1944) featured a *Vogue* cover taken by Horst.
Taken: New York, 1947

Plate 80, TALLULAH BANKHEAD (1903-68)

Born in Huntsville, Alabama, the daughter of the Speaker of the House of Representatives, Bankhead was one of America's most brilliant stage actresses. Known for her tempestuous personality and uninhibited behaviour, she first made her reputation on the London stage after travelling to England in 1923 and starring in various productions in the following seven years. Her film career was less memorable though she was cited by the New York Film Critics for her performance in Alfred Hitchcock's *Lifeboat* (1944).
Taken: New York, 1940s

Plate 81, OLIVIER MESSIAEN (1908-92)

Messiaen cut a giant, if controversial figure in twentieth-century European music. This portrait, taken for *Vogue* in celebration of a musical revival in post-war France, accompanied pictures of Poulenc and Barraud as evidence. '[Messiaen's] work', said *Vogue*, 'is filled with unexpected rhythms, dissonant harmonies. He looks like a school teacher, is a church organist and Professor of Harmony at the Paris Conservatoire.' He was imprisoned in Silesia during the war, during which time he never lost his beliefs: 'Above all, I am a Catholic musician ... all my works are an act of faith'.
Taken: Paris, 1946
Published: American *Vogue*, June 1946, p.160

Plate 82, GERTRUDE STEIN (1874-1946)

An American, Gertrude Stein was a famous literary figure in Paris. Her *Autobiography of Alice B. Toklas* is considered a masterpiece (Toklas was her life-long companion). However, *Vanity Fair* once named her as one of its 'Ten Dullest Authors'. She was a magnet for expatriate writers, among them Ezra Pound and Ernest Hemingway, and a patron of painters such as Picasso and Gris. At the end of the war (it was the second she had lived through in France), Stein sat for Horst for over

two days. The first sitting took place in the atelier of Pierre Balmain, as part of Horst's coverage of the collections for *Vogue*. Stein and the couturier had become great friends during the occupation of France, and Balmain arranged for Horst to photograph her and her poodle, Basket, in her own apartment the following day. She was also sketched there by Eric, the *Vogue* fashion illustrator. The portrait of Basket on the wall behind Stein is by Marie Laurençin and the lampshade designed by Picasso. The sketch was published in *Vogue* with the following tribute to the distinguished American in Paris: 'Gertrude Stein is respected by French intellectuals and by American GIs because she took the trouble to talk to them.' Janet Flanner remarked that the portrait was 'the most beautiful photograph of any man I have ever seen'.
Taken: In Stein's apartment, Paris, 1946

Plate 83, JEAN COCTEAU (1889-1963)

Of all the figures that came and went during Horst's Parisian days, both before and after the war, none loomed quite as large and so frequently as Cocteau. 'Anything Cocteau did or said was stimulating,' recalled Horst. 'He taught me about France, about the theatre and how to look at life. He walked through the street and suddenly something would happen.' Cocteau was chiefly a dramatist and film-maker but, true to the spirit of the times in which he flourished, he could turn his hand (he was very proud of his long-fingered hands) to almost anything and succeed. And succeed he did, in fashion illustration, poetry, novels, journalism for *Paris-Soir* and of course the dispensing of *bons mots*: 'Genius in art', he declared, 'consists in knowing how far we may go too far.' He was notoriously and semi-permanently unwell due to a mixture of nerves, unsuccessful love affairs and an addiction to opium. Strangely in all the years of their friendship, Horst only ever took one photograph of Cocteau. It was this one tucked away on the last frame at the end of a roll of film. Horst was on assignment in Venice and had just photographed Cocteau's friend and patroness Misia Sert.
Taken: Venice, 1947

Plate 84, MISIA SERT (1872-1950)

The widow of the Spanish painter José Maria Sert, Misia Sert was photographed by Horst in the Café Florian in Venice on her last trip to the city, three years before she died. She was a hugely influential person in Parisian life of the 1920s without ever doing anything other than pronouncing judgement, and her approval was sought by Picasso, Diaghilev, Cocteau and Stravinsky. 'A fascinating cross', wrote Lawford, 'between an angel and a tigress.' She led an enchanted life, though it started inauspiciously in a hotel room in St Petersburg where her mother lay dying after childbirth. She was painted by Vuillard, Toulouse-Lautrec, Renoir (eight times) and Bonnard. Verlaine and Mallarmé dedicated poems to her and she counted Nijinsky, Ravel and Debussy among her friends. Horst remembered that her apartment on the rue de Rivoli was 'fantastic ... she had extraordinary taste, but the most extraordinary objects were these rock crystal pyramids'. Erik Satie, who knew her well, described her as 'a lovely cat – so hide your fish ...'

Taken: In the north corner of the Café Florian, Venice, 1947
Published: American *Vogue*, 15 December 1947, p.181

Plate 85, JEAN MARAIS (1913-98)

To Jean Cocteau, Marais was lover, protégé and inspiration, appearing in many of his plays, poems and artworks. But it is as the striking leading man in films such as *La Belle et la Bête* (1946), *Les Parents Terribles* (1948), *Orphée* (1949) and *Le Testament d'Orphée* (1959) that he became known outside France. He was born in Cherbourg to a veterinary surgeon and a career shoplifter (the infant Marais acted as look-out). He trained as a photographer before meeting Cocteau in 1937. They were inseparable for nearly quarter of a century until Cocteau's death. Rejected by France's leading drama schools and possessing, as he admitted himself, a 'thin voice' and questionable technique, it wasn't expected that his career would survive without Cocteau's patronage. In time, however, he became a Grand Old Man of French theatre, undertaking roles such as Lear, Prospero and as Nero in Racine's *Britannicus*. He also worked with Abel Gance, Visconti, Jean Renoir and Jacques Demy. During the occupation of France, his athleticism and 'Aryan' looks proved popular with both sides, though some journalists tried to disparage him as 'a weathercock of the third sex', although he earned the Croix de Guerre as a soldier in the French army. After the war, he appeared in a series of swashbuckling epics and at one point played the Leslie Charteris character, 'the Saint'. Cocteau's infatuation produced some memorable low points, including casting his protégé in lederhosen for *L'Aigle a Deux Têtes* (1948), but Marais was loyal enough to revive *Les Parents Terrible* (playing the father this time round not the son). Bernardo Bertolucci gave Marais his final film role as an ageing art historian in *Stealing Beauty* (1996). His was a charmed existence which he lived to the full and never forgot his good fortune: 'Life', he told one French newspaper, 'is unfair. I got nothing but the best.'
Taken: In Marais' studio, 1950s

Plate 86, DIAMANTE BOSCHETTI

For a *Vogue* feature on Venetian society, this is one of the rare occasions that Horst disregarded conventional wisdom and worked with both children and animals. Diamante Boschetti was the infant daughter of Count and Countess Luling Boschetti. *Vogue* did not disclose the name of her little dog. The text accompanying the photograph revealed that it was less about the figures in the foreground than the shimmering perspective behind them. The Boschetti family owned one of the most spectacular Palladian villas in private hands, the Villa Barbaro. Decorated by Veronese, the paintings were still luminous centuries after their creation. Many were executed in a *trompe l'œil* style, the artist having left, in one tableau, his work-shoes and paint brush. 'Except for the red damask-hung master bedrooms,' reported *Vogue*, 'the house repeats the watery blues and greens of the frescoes which seem to bring landscape, sky and cypresses into every room.'
Taken: In the Great Hall of the Villa Barbaro, Venice, 1947
Published: American *Vogue*, 15 December 1947, p.178

Plate 87, CARLOS CHAVEZ (1899-1978)

The celebrated composer and conductor was photographed by Horst on a trip to Mexico in 1946. Horst also photographed, among others, the painters Tamayo, Rivera and Siqueiros, all of whom appeared in a *Vogue* feature on the country's cultural climate. Chavez's *œuvre* consists of opera as well as symphonies and concertos, and several ballet scores. Apart from some piano tuition, he was mainly self-taught and was much influenced by Mexican-Indian culture, which lent his symphonies a distinctive sound. As a conductor he led many notable orchestras across America, Latin America and Europe. He established the first permanent Mexican Symphony Orchestra and 'made it great' according to *Vogue*. He was asked to plan what eventually became The National Institute of Fine Arts for Mexico. He was particularly fêted in the United States, where he made lifelong friendships with Aaron Copeland and Edgar Varese, and in 1958 he was offered the Norton Chair of Poetics at Harvard.
Taken: Mexico, 1946; published 1 April 1946

Plate 88, DIEGO RIVERA (1886-1957)

Horst vacationed with Huene in Mexico after signing his first *Vogue* contract after the war. Through the *Vogue* contributor Miguel Covarrubias, Horst had met the painter José Clemente Orozco and photographed him. He wished to complete the triumvirate of Mexican painters well known at the time and went in search of David Alfaro Siqueiros and Diego Rivera. The first was easier to find than the second – who was in hiding from the government. The result was this montage of photographs of the famous Mexican-Indian muralist, some with his partner, the legendary Frida Kahlo. Rivera had spent time in Europe and had known Picasso, Apollinaire and Cézanne and was influenced by 'Cubism and Communism'. (He was a colleague and sympathizer of Trotsky.) In the early 1930s he was commissioned to design the murals for the Rockefeller Center, New York. Virtually completed, the mural was rejected and destroyed because Rivera had included in it a portrait of Lenin.
Taken: Mexico, 1941 (montaged later)
Published: American *Vogue*, 1 April 1946, p.156 (portrait only)

Plate 89, VALENTINE LAWFORD (1911-91)

Valentine Lawford, occasionally known as 'Nicholas', was Horst's lifelong companion at Oyster Bay, his biographer and textual collaborator on at least three books of Horst's photographs. He also wrote the lengthy articles to accompany Horst's interiors photographs for *Vogue*. 'Mr Lawford's style', remarked the *New York Times*, 'is as elegant and seemingly effortless as Mr Horst's best photographs.' The son of a naval officer, Lawford attended the Universities of Cambridge, Strasbourg and the Sorbonne in Paris. For sixteen years he was a member of the Diplomatic Corps at the Foreign Office, where he served as Assistant Private Secretary to three Secretaries of State for Foreign Affairs: Lord Halifax, Anthony Eden and Ernest Bevin. He was described by Henry 'Chips' Channon as 'a rather Second Empire Secretary' and Sir John Colville as 'a clever and amusing diplomat'. During the war he was an interpreter to both Churchill and de Gaulle and attended the Moscow, Yalta and Quebec conferences. He was pursued by the hostess and *grande dame* Emerald Cunard, but settled with Horst in 1950 on leaving the Diplomatic Service. As a writer he contributed not only to *Vogue* (the American, French and Italian editions), but also to *Cornhill Magazine*, *House and Garden* and *Architectural Digest*. As a painter he was known for his landscapes and flower portraits. His memoirs, entitled *Bound for Diplomacy*, were published in 1963.

Taken: Mapperton House, Dorset, 1948

Plate 90, SIR OSBERT SITWELL (1892-1969)

Eclipsed as a poet by his sister Edith, Sir Osbert found fame for his celebrated five-volume series of memoirs, *Left Hand, Right Hand*. He inherited the Sitwell baronetcy, the estate of Renishaw and the castle of Montegufoni near Florence on the death of his father. He spent much of the last years of his life at Montegufoni, an eccentric if kindly Englishman abroad, and enjoyed increasing recognition as an English comedic genius. A lifelong friend, the writer Violet Trefusis wrote shortly after his death: 'Everything to do with Osbert filled me with awe: his magnificent ancestral home Renishaw, his dim and mysterious mother, his unknown ogre of a father (who turned out to resemble Titian's portrait of Charles V with his foxy little red beard), his fascinating but intimidating sister Edith who made me feel uncouth and ungraceful ...' With Edith, he joined Horst and Valentine Lawford for a lunch party at Oyster Bay to meet Greta Garbo and was only slightly put out that lunch was delayed while she took a walk round the garden.

Taken: 1948

Plate 91, LISA FONSSAGRIVES (1911-92)

Taken: 1951

Plate 92, IRVING PENN (b.1917)

A colleague of Horst at *Vogue* for over fifty years, Penn started out as assistant to the Art Director, Alexander Liberman in 1943. He championed Penn's highly stylized representations of feminine beauty, which have to a great extent defined the art of couture at its most opulent and, arguably, at its most inventive. Of all his starkly composed black-and-white *œuvre*, perhaps his photographs of the Paris collections of 1950 best represent his contribution to the early post-war ideal of feminine poise, glamour and chic. His best fashion work was made in collaboration with his wife Lisa Fonssagrives, his muse and model, an early favourite of Horst. His portraits for *Vogue* of writers, artists, stage and film actors and ballet stars have a compelling quality and often posterity has proved Penn's photographs to be the definitive representation of a sitter. They transcend the pages of the monthly magazine to find themselves on the walls of the world's major museums. His still lifes, famously of cigarette butts and other street detritus, and his championing of the platinum-palladium print also rank high in the list of his contributions to the cultural life of the twentieth and twenty-first centuries. The antithesis of a 'snapshot' aesthetic, Penn has never left anything to chance and his rigidly composed and formal photographs, whether of clothes, celebrities or of tribespeople from Papua New Guinea to Peru, resonate long after in the mind. He still works regularly for *Vogue*, investing his photographs with a solemnity and graphic clarity which few can match. He has maintained that the camera is merely 'a tool' but 'the situation is magical. I stand in awe of it'.

Taken: New York, 1951

Plate 93, LUCIA BOSÉ (b.1931)

Horst said she had the look of 'a continental Louise Brooks'. A former Miss Italy (of 1947) Lucia Bosé made the transition from beauty pageant to cinema screen. Her success did not lie in Hollywood, but with European intellectuals and *auteurs*; her first appearance was in *No Peace Among the Olives* (1950) by Giuseppe de Santis. Her art-house credentials were secured with roles in the films of Antonioni, Buñuel and Fellini. She had a small part in Cocteau's *Le Testament d'Orphée* and knew Visconti and Jeanne Moreau. Her movie profile was correspondingly low, not least because she was wife to the flamboyant, tempestuous, charismatic matador Luis Miguel Dominguin, who throughout the 1950s exemplified the artistry of the *corrida* and drank coffee laced with cognac for breakfast. Horst met her at lunch with Visconti and was so taken with her beauty that he photographed her right away.

Taken: Rome, 1952

Published: American *Vogue*, 15 August, 1953, p.153 (variant pose)

Plate 94, ALBERTO MORAVIA (1907-90)

Arguably the most famous Italian author of the last century, Moravia was no stranger to controversy, let alone the obscenity courts for most of his working life. He dissected in a clean, precise style the bourgeois manners and morals of decadent Roman society to popular, if controversial, success. His first novel, *Time of Indifference*, published in 1929, was 'discouraged' by the Fascist authorities. *The Fancy Dress Party* (1941) ridiculed Mussolini, who promptly had it banned outright. *Women of Rome* (1947) concerned a young woman's descent into vice. *Time of Desecration* (1979) had a charge of obscenity brought against it. Moravia wrote the film script for Bertolucci's *Last Tango in Paris* (1972, also the subject of a censorship debate) but he then decided that the actors should improvise their lines. Horst photographed Moravia at Visconti's insistence. 'I had heard of his books, but I hadn't read any. The whole thing took ten minutes.' Years later, Moravia revealed to *Vogue* that he hated having his picture taken because 'it makes me feel reduced to an object'. He also hated his own face because 'probably I have a feeling that I should be different. You always have inside yourself a different face.'

Taken: Rome, 1957

Plate 95, HERBERT VON KARAJAN (1908-89)

The austere conductor was photographed informally at leisure in Kitzbühel, Austria. Horst noted that von Karajan oversaw the Salzburg Festival in terrifying detail. While in Salzburg, von Karajan once got into a cab and on being asked 'Where to?' by

the driver, replied, 'It doesn't matter. I have things to do everywhere'. *Vogue* said that he was a musical director of 'such scope that he makes the tyrannies of Toscanini and Koussevitsky seem like mere tempers'. Fired from the Vienna State Opera after a power struggle, he was made permanent Director of the Berlin Philharmonic. *Vogue* noted that 'he pilots his own turboprop plane, drives his jag and motor launch and sails his boat, skis superbly at St Moritz with his beautiful wife Eliette'.
Taken: Kitzbühel, Austria, 1958

Plate 96, ELIETTE VON KARAJAN

Eliette Mouret, born and brought up in the South of France, spent her early career as a fashion model, particularly as a house-model for Dior. She met von Karajan, twenty-eight years her senior, in St Tropez and became his third wife in October 1958. They had two daughters, Isabel (b.1960) and Arabel (b.1964). Eliette von Karajan, a watercolourist, is now a leading figure in the major charitable foundation set up in 1986 by von Karajan, three years before he died, for the promotion of the arts.
Taken: Kitzbühel, Austria, 1958

Plate 97, DWIGHT D. EISENHOWER (1890-1969) AND HIS WIFE MAMIE (GENEVA DOUD; 1896-1979)

Horst photographed the distinguished general and his wife, Mamie, on the eve of his election to the White House in 1952. The Republican candidate, he won by a large majority. His tenure in Washington was marked by a preoccupation with foreign policy, in particular with a combative approach towards Communism and the beginning of the cold war with the USSR. A military hero and a brilliant strategist during World War II, he led the Allied Forces in North Africa. In 1944 he was appointed Supreme Commander for the cross-channel attack on occupied France with 'Operation Overlord'.
Reluctant to push on to Berlin, he allowed Russia to occupy it first, which, coupled with his tacit approval for the immediate dismantling of the Allied groundforces, led to Russia's pre-eminence as the leading military power in Europe.
Eisenhower was instrumental in the construction of NATO in the post-war years, before relinquishing his post as Supreme Commander to run for the presidency. Horst was a favourite of incumbents at the White House; the first president he photographed in office was Harry S. Truman in 1945.
Taken: 1952
Published: American *Vogue*, 1 November 1952, p. 94; British *Vogue*, December 1952, p.88

Plate 98, JACQUELINE BOUVIER KENNEDY (1929-94) AND HER SISTER LEE RADZIWILL (b.1933)

Horst took this informal fashion photograph of the legendary Bouvier sisters for a feature entitled 'American Sisters in Sweaters' (the other sisters featured were Evelyn and Patricia Bates). When Edna Woolman Chase resigned from American *Vogue* in 1952, she was succeeded by her deputy, Jessica Daves, who Horst remembered as clear-headed and practical, with a shrewd grasp of the business of mid-century American

fashion. She immediately substituted for Mrs Chase's simplicity and respect for European art and culture a no-nonsense policy of promoting all things American. To that end she produced bi-annual 'Americana' issues of which the fashion pages comprised uninspiring collections of joyful-hearted cardiganed girl students bicycling to doughnut shops. This is one of Horst's less half-hearted attempts at realizing Daves' vision. Horst spent much of Daves' decade-long tenure travelling abroad and working for *House and Garden* before being asked back in 1962 to work with Daves' successor, the exotic Diana Vreeland. Jacqueline Bouvier eventually became First Lady at the White House and perhaps the most famous American woman of her time. Her sister Lee married Michael T. Canfield and then Prince Stanislas Radziwill and most recently, Herbert Ross. Horst photographed for *Vogue* their magnificent house, Turville Grange, in the Thames Valley in Buckinghamshire. Mrs Kennedy's sweater was by Goldworm, Mrs Canfield's by Garland. Of the few photographs Horst kept at home, one was of Jacqueline Kennedy.
Taken: New York, 1955
Published: American *Vogue*, 15 March 1955, p.127

Plate 99, MARIA CALLAS (1923-77)

This is the full version of Horst's portrait. Usually it is reproduced as a full frame headshot, cropped off at the neck, taken in her suite at the Waldorf Astoria, New York. At the time neither version was published by *Vogue*, who commissioned the photographs. This is Horst's memory of the sitting from *Horst: His Work and His World*: 'What a face! Callas hadn't wanted to come to the studio. I went to the Waldorf with Margaret Case, then Social Editor of *Vogue*. Margaret mentioned Elsa Maxwell and Callas said "Don't mention that name to me!" ... You really felt her temper. I felt lucky to get out of there alive. Hers was the most changeable of moods. It all came from inside – moods, temper, and charm too, and also boredom, impatience. You felt the violence and at the same time the beauty, and all this is in a split second. When I look at this photograph I say "How the hell did I ever do it?"'
Taken: New York, 1952

Plate 100, PRINCESS COLONNA

Princess Colonna hailed from an ancient and distinguished Roman dynasty, their name taken from a small village in the Alban hills. The Colonna family have, over the centuries, produced a Pope (Martin V), as well as statesmen and scholars, generals and cardinals.
Taken: Rome, 1952

Plate 101, DAME SYBIL THORNDIKE (1882-1976) AND SIR LEWIS CASSON (1875-1969)

By the time Horst took this photograph in New York, Thorndike and Casson had been married for forty years, had spent fifty years on the stage between them and had each played more than one thousand roles. The couple also found time to write a biography of Lillian Bayliss together. Dame Sybil was the greatest stage actress of her time (with over

one hundred Shakespearean roles alone to her credit) and as a producer, Casson created the milieu for his wife to flourish in. Their greatest success was undoubtedly Bernard Shaw's *Saint Joan*, written with Thorndike in mind, in which they both acted and Casson also directed. It opened in 1924, was revived in 1931 and in Thorndike's long lifetime she is reckoned to have played the title role two thousand times across the globe. *Vogue* commissioned this joint portrait from Horst but published another, less sparse, version. Now the actors were appearing on Broadway in Graham Greene's *The Potting Shed*. The magazine noted that their early repertory company had glorious alumni – Laurence Olivier and Carol Reed held her train in a 1925 production of *Henry VIII*. 'Dame Sybil,' it continued, 'a vibrant woman with lapis-lazuli blue eyes and Sir Lewis, rockily British and erect, appear, off stage, a tea-cosy couple interested in their ten grandchildren.' 'On stage', said Dame Sybil, 'we argue like hell.'
Taken: In *The Potting Shed*, New York, 1957
Published: American *Vogue*, February 1957, p.60

Plate 102, KATINA PAXINOU (1900-73)
Paxinou was the leading Greek tragedienne of her day and for the previous four decades too, having made her debut in Athens in 1924. Apart from the great classical roles, she was an accomplished interpreter of Shakespeare and Ibsen. She also won an Oscar for her performance as 'La Pasionaria' in *For Whom the Bell Tolls* (1943). Horst took this portrait for *Vogue*; the published one showed Paxinou with her male counterpart, the actor and tragedian Alexis Minotis. He would later direct Maria Callas in a version of *Medea* at Covent Garden. Set in the ruins beneath the Acropolis in the theatre of Herod Atticus, Paxinou played for Horst's camera a scene from Sophocles' *Electra*, tears streaming down her face.
Taken: Athens, 1955

Plate 103, LOUISE DE VILMORIN (1902-69)
Horst first photographed Louise de Vilmorin in 1937, playing a guitar, when she was regarded as one of the most beautiful women of her day. A poet, novelist and musician, she was also a renowned hostess. A born raconteuse, she was, as Horst put it, 'one of those women only France produce: an enchantress....' She was a true *femme fatale*; it was said that once when she refused a marriage proposal on a boat on the Thames, the poor young suitor threw himself overboard. Perhaps with this in mind, *Vogue* asked her to write on 'What Makes a Man Memorable?' She married twice, to Leigh Hunt, a descendant of the great English poet, and then to a Hungarian count, Paul Pálffy. Sadly she died before marrying her third husband-to-be, André Malraux. She wrote the novel *The Earrings of Madame De*, which Max Ophuls turned into a film, her poems were set to music by Poulenc, and her friends included everyone worth knowing in Paris including, inevitably, Chanel and Cocteau. For Horst's friend Visconti, she translated numerous American plays into French. When Horst met her in Paris again after the war, they dined on the Place d'Odéon. He was disturbed to find she had brought with her a child's coffin, which contained the

manuscript of some poems that she requested Horst to illustrate, but he declined.
Taken: Verriers, France, 1958

Plate 104, INGRID BERGMAN (1915-82)
The third time Horst photographed Bergman was in Paris in the year of her film *The Inn of the Sixth Happiness*. She had long established her career and popularity at this stage. He had also photographed her in 1958, two years after *Anastasia*. On the day of the sitting Edmonde Charles-Roux of French *Vogue* brought her a bunch of yellow roses, saying 'This is just to remind you.' Horst never found out what it was intended she should be reminded of, but he wrote, 'Ingrid remained still. She said nothing, and turned her back to me as if to pull herself together. Her face was tight, disturbed ... it was upsetting to see her like that. I don't know what I said to relax her. Her humanity, her kindness and warmth were overwhelming – no affectation of any sort.'
Taken: Paris, 1959
Published: American *Vogue*, 1 November 1959, p.127 (variant pose)

Plate 105, MME JACQUES BALSAN (CONSUELO VANDERBILT, DUCHESS OF MARLBOROUGH) (1876-1964)
A neighbour of Horst's on Long Island, Mme Balsan was a legendary beauty, with an almost Proustian life story. Christian Bérard almost passed out with delirium on discovering that she was to be seated in the row in front of him and Horst at the Opera. She was a Vanderbilt by birth and in 1895 married the 9th Duke of Marlborough in *the* society match of its day. Her second marriage was to Jacques Balsan, a French airforce officer, and they settled in Paris. They fled to New York when France was occupied and divided their time between their estates on Long Island and near Palm Beach and their apartment on Park Avenue. Horst was introduced to her through Valentine Lawford and they got on well, despite the former Duchess's ambivalence towards Germans, which dated from having to entertain the last Kaiser and Crown Prince at Blenheim. She found, according to Lawford, that Horst's voice and accent were pitched a little low for her hearing-aid to comfortably receive. On his first visit, Horst took many photographs of her Florida house and its legendary paintings (by Utrillo, Fragonard, Cézanne, Renoir among others) and its equally celebrated gardens. *House and Garden* asked him to take more, followed by *Vogue*. A decade after that, *Vogue* asked him to take pictures of a house she had bought at Southampton. When Diana Vreeland became Editor of *Vogue*, she asked Horst again to photograph Mme Balsan and her house, in one of the first of the interiors commissions that would herald a change in the direction of his magazine photography. Lawford was assigned to write an accompanying text: 'Horst was told to photograph ... her door handles, her flowers, her plates, her knives and forks and the bathroom details – even the soap ... I was to describe in-depth the refinement of her taste.'
Taken: Oyster Bay, Long Island, 1952

Published: American *Vogue*, 1 November 1952, p.122

Plate 106, SUZY PARKER (b.1932)

The flame-haired model with a temperament to match, Suzy Parker was one of Horst's favourite models. Parker always enlivened otherwise routine fashion pictures for Horst. By this time his heart was perhaps not in fashion, having become disenchanted with a new regime at *Vogue*. Yet Horst's first impression of Parker was not encouraging: 'The first time I photographed her she couldn't keep still ... so I just walked out.' After half an hour the *Vogue* editor begged him to return. '[Suzy] had been crying and was still drying her tears. She looked like a scolded child, but pulled herself together bravely. And that was the start of our great friendship.' This picture was taken for a 'Modess ... because' campaign in Kitzbühel, Austria. Horst's disenchantment had led to more advertising work, rather than editorial. 'This was Suzy's first trip to Europe,' recalled Horst, 'it was a brand-new world for her. She was wonderful, easy, uninhibited....' In Austria she caused a sensation and crowds followed her to each location. Parker said of the shoot, 'my feet were cold in ten feet of snow in those ridiculous wire-mesh boots that I had to wear ... When Horst exclaimed, as he often did, "How well she looks today!" he was referring not to me but to his odious little dachshund Mabel.' Suzy Parker later became an actress and Horst joked that maybe she would do for the movies what she never did for him – hold still.

Taken: Kitzbühel, Austria, 1952, for the 'Modess ... because' campaign

Plates 107 and 108, VERUSCHKA, COUNTESS VERA VON LEHNDORFF (b.1939)

One of the most famous models in magazine history, Veruschka was also one of the tallest (at 6'1") and, along with Princess Natasha Paley, one of the most aristocratic. Born Countess Vera von Lehndorff, she was the daughter of Count Heinrich von Lehndorff-Steinort, who was executed for his part in the Stauffenberg plot to kill Hitler. She became a model after studying art, and although it was too exotic a consideration to begin with, it was under Diana Vreeland's aegis at American *Vogue* and her relentless pursuit of the off-kilter that Veruschka's star ascended. In collaboration with the photographer Franco Rubartelli, she metamorphosized into anything *Vogue* wanted her to be: a leopard in a tree, an alien landing at the North Pole, a shimmering, golden mermaid, a coral-encrusted sea nymph. She can be seen writhing for David Hemming's lens in Antonioni's *Blow Up* (1966) and later in Hulger Trülzsch's *trompe l'œil* photographs; body-painted out of recognition as a stone, a leaf, an animal or the side of a warehouse wall. Horst was one of the first to capture Veruschka's lithe exoticism for American *Vogue*, in a *plein air* style redolent of the *Nachtkultur* of the photographer's youth.

Taken: Hawaii, 1965

Published: *Vogue Pattern Book*, June-July 1965

Plate 109, STEVE McQUEEN (1930-80)

In fast-paced films like *The Getaway* (1972), Steve McQueen was the screen personification of effortless cool. He brought a self-deprecating nonchalance to his role as the 'Cooler King' in his best-known film, *The Great Escape* (1963); his abortive escape to freedom on a motorbike its most famous moment. As an actor, he also mixed the easy charm with a little gravitas, having begun some time in prison himself as a juvenile delinquent and having served as a Marine. His burning presence in *Hell is for Heroes* (1962) and *The Thomas Crown Affair* (1968) was so charismatic that his acting hardly appeared to matter. As the writer James Wolcott put it, admiringly, in *Vanity Fair*: 'His monotone has a sneaky approach. He speaks as if trying to be overheard rather than heard ...' Horst photographed the proto-action hero for the *Men in Vogue* section of the magazine, which noted that Steve McQueen 'comes just the way you might hope – cool, hip, easy, very much his own man'. He came complete with the argot of times; on clothes: 'I used to play it down, but now it's the time of the swinger....' On cars, which on the screen he was seldom out of: 'its my other big bag ... but when I get uptight I go out and drive my bike' (a Triumph 650cc). Unlike his rival, Beaton, Horst did not approach the 1960s as a neo-Dandy with a glamorous past. He concentrated on the interiors and possessions of celebrities rather than their likenesses, only rarely taking 'straight' portraits at this time. Thus Horst and 'groovy' ought to be strange bedfellows, but as this picture and the contact sheets show, he got Steve McQueen's insouciance just about right.

Taken: San Francisco, 1967

Published: American *Vogue*, 1 March 1967, p.135

Plate 110, JENNIFER O'NEILL (b.1947)

Before embarking on a career as an actress, Jennifer O'Neill was a highly successful model and was photographed in this capacity by Horst at Oyster Bay. She had started modelling in order to save up for a horse (she now owns a stables complex in Nashville). The fashion photographer Scavullo once said of her: 'I'd look at her in the studio and the sun would come through the window and hit her face and I'd get weak all over.' A famous face on the cover of *Cosmopolitan*, she had a long association with Cover Girl cosmetics. As an actress, she first appeared in Howard Hawks' *Rio Lobo* (1970), but it was her next film, *Summer of '42* (1971), that catapulted her into the limelight. Her portrait of the 'older woman' in the coming-of-age movie made her an object of worship for a generation of lovesick adolescents. After that, she starred in largely forgettable films such as *Caravans* (1978) with Anthony Quinn, Blake Edwards' *The Carey Treatment* (1972) and *The Reincarnation of Peter Proud* (1975). She appeared briefly in some interesting films including Cronenberg's *Scanners* (1981) and Visconti's last film, *L'Innocente* (1976). Her autobiography, *Surviving Myself*, is a testament to her triumph over adversity. She has been married nine times, had nine miscarriages, attempted suicide as a teenager, undergone electroconvulsive therapy, broken her neck and back in a riding accident and shot herself accidentally in the hip. 'And that', she has said, 'was just the tip of the iceberg.'

Taken: In a silvered suit by Norman Norell, 1964

Published: American *Vogue*, 15 December 1964, pp.100-101

Plate 111, CY TWOMBLY (b.1928)

The American painter has spent much of his life abroad. After travelling with his friend, the painter Robert Rauschenberg, for several months to North Africa, Spain and Italy, he settled in Rome in 1956. From there, closer to the classical civilization and mythology that have influenced his paintings and occasional sculptures, he has pursued the abstract scratches, doodles and scrawls, often on an immense scale, that have made his international reputation. *Fifty Days at Iliam* (1978) is a ten-part work inspired by the *Iliad* of Homer. For a large interiors feature for *Vogue*, Horst photographed Twombly, his wife Tatiana (descended from the Borgias, according to Horst) and his 6-year-old son in their apartment in Rome, filled with busts and statues of figures from Greek and Roman mythology: 'When I photographed him', said Horst, 'he was hardly known to the New York art world. But Castelli exhibited his paintings and today his work hangs in American and European museums.' Alongside Jackson Pollock, he is perhaps one of the most influential painters in the European avant-garde movement from the 1960s onwards. In this photograph Twombly is wearing a World War I leather greatcoat and the car is a 1928 Alfa Romeo, which he occasionally took to car rallies.
Taken: Rome, 1966
Published: American *Vogue*, 15 November 1966, p.184

Plate 112, FRANCO ZEFFIRELLI (b.1923)

Horst met Zeffirelli at the same lunch party given by Visconti where he met and photographed Lucia Bosé. Zeffirelli, a former architecture student and actor, had just designed the sets and costumes for Visconti's production of *A Streetcar Named Desire*. Photographing him years later, Horst said of the young Italian, 'He directed the photograph. I did what he told me, every little detail. "You click the camera when I tell you to ...".' A decade after that Horst photographed him, again for *Vogue*, in his country retreat near Positano, Italy, revealing that Zeffirelli was a keen gardener and cultivator of 'fruit trees, herbs and vegetables in abundance'. Though known for decades as a designer of plays and opera, a master of colour and detail, he turned to directing and producing them (memorably working with Maria Callas). His operas, in particular, are noted for their extravagance. In 1967 he directed his first feature film, *The Taming of the Shrew*, and followed it a year later with *Romeo and Juliet*, which won Oscars for cinematography and costume design. His sumptuous adaptations for the big screen include *La Traviata* (1982) and *Hamlet* (1990). His most recent film is *Tea with Mussolini* (1999), a semi-fictionalized account of his boyhood during World War II.
Taken: New York, 1964

Plate 113, W.H. AUDEN (1907-73)

A giant of twentieth-century literature, Auden rivals perhaps only T.S. Eliot as the most influential English-language poet of his time. Though his poems can be oblique and abstruse (especially his earlier work), he enjoyed a posthumous popular revival when *Funeral Blues*, one of his more accessible poems, was featured in the film *Four Weddings and a Funeral* (1994). Having

left Oxford, where he had forged friendships with fellow poets Louis MacNeice and Cecil Day-Lewis, he spent a year in Berlin. There, he was joined by a schoolfriend, Christopher Isherwood, whose experiences of life in the city gave rise to his 'Berlin' trilogy of novels. Auden's first book of poems was published privately in 1928 by his friend Stephen Spender in an edition of around fifty. After working as a schoolmaster and private tutor, Auden's first commercially available volume *Poems* was published. He joined the film unit of the British General Post Office, where his spoken verse commentary for the documentary *Night Mail* (1936) elevated it to a classic. Aligning himself to the left during the Spanish Civil War, he duly made a trip there to experience the conflict at first hand. In 1939, on the eve of World War II, he left Britain for the United States, where he spent much of the rest of his life, becoming a citizen in 1946. *Another Time* was published in 1940, regarded by many as his masterpiece and from which came *Funeral Blues* and the well-known *Musée des Beaux-Arts*. In collaboration with Chester Kallman, he wrote libretti for Stravinsky and Benjamin Britten among others. In 1970 Horst photographed Auden in New York City, where he had made his home since his arrival in America (Isherwood settled in California). Two years after the portrait was taken he left again for England, where he died in 1973.
Taken: New York, 1970

Plate 114, LOUISE BROOKS (1906-85)

By the time this portrait was taken, Louise Brooks, darling of the silent era, was living in reduced circumstances and all but forgotten. Horst photographed her here for *Life* magazine (and was subsequently included in the book *Return Engagement*) in her tiny apartment in Rochester, New York, where she had lived since 1956. The daughter of a lawyer, and a mother with a *laissez-faire* attitude, Brooks trained as a dancer. She achieved fame in the 1920s with films made in Germany for G.W. Pabst including the classic *Pandora's Box*, and *Diary of a Lost Girl*. In 1931, due to her difficult attitude, her American film career foundered. She became a dancer again at the Plaza Hotel and for a time took a job as a clerk at the department store Saks Fifth Avenue. She subsisted in her apartment, living off an allowance from a wealthy benefactor. After the sitting was over, James Watters recalled a letter she wrote explaining why quite so many people had gathered for Horst's allegedly private photo session: 'She had invited friends and a local newspaper reporter ("just starey people") to watch Horst. "I wanted them here to keep me from remembering that I am an old hag in front of the camera; I wanted the reporter for a piece in the paper which might impress my landlord to the point of giving me a new stove".'
Taken: Rochester, New York, 1979

Plate 115, KATHARINE HEPBURN (b.1907)

Since Horst's first encounter with Hepburn in Hollywood in 1935, she had won two further Oscars for her parts in *Guess Who's Coming to Dinner* (1967) and *The Lion in Winter* (1968). Hepburn had also received a record eight other Oscar nominations for her parts in such classics as *The Philadelphia*

Story (1940) and the 1942 film *Woman of the Year* (during which she began a lifelong partnership with Spencer Tracy). She also made *The African Queen* (1951), *Summertime* (1955) and *Suddenly Last Summer* (1959). Hepburn continued to work well into the 1980s, her final triumph being her part in *On Golden Pond* (1981) with Henry and Jane Fonda.
Taken: New York, 1981

Plate 116, ARTHUR MILLER (b.1915)

One of the twentieth century's greatest dramatists, Arthur Miller was born in New York City. After high school he marked time in a succession of jobs as a clerk, a truck driver and a dishwasher, which eventually enabled him to pay his way through college. He began a succession of plays, including his first on Broadway in 1944, *The Man Who Had All the Luck*, which culminated in the huge success of *All My Sons* (1947). It earned him a Critics' Circle award and placed him at the forefront of American playwrights. But it was *Death of a Salesman*, written in six weeks the following year, that made his name throughout the world, earning Miller a Pulitzer Prize for Theatre; it was later filmed. *The Crucible* (1953), also filmed, cemented his reputation with its scathing indictment of contemporary political persecution in the 'McCarthy' years, which he mirrored in his reworking of the historical witch trials of Salem, Massachusetts. Other notable successes were *A View from the Bridge* (1955), *After the Fall* (1963) and *A Ride Down Mount Morgan* (1991). He encountered another kind of publicity from his marriage, as Marilyn Monroe's third husband. She appeared in the film of his script *The Misfits* (1961) and they were divorced in the same year.
Taken: 1980

Plate 117, PALOMA PICASSO (b.1949)

In 1978 Francine Crescent, Editor-in-Chief of French *Vogue*, requested Horst to photograph the Paris Collections again for the first time since the 1950s. Then and subsequently, it became a high point of his [later] professional years: 'I have simply done what I did forty years ago ... tried to convey a beautiful image....' In Paris, the magazine booked him into the Hôtel de Bourgogne et Montana, within walking distance of his pre-war home on the rue Saint-Roman. This photograph, ostensibly a portrait of Paloma Picasso, is in fact a fashion picture. She is wearing an ensemble designed by Yves Saint-Laurent. In subsequent exposures, she wears clothes by Karl Lagerfeld. The shoot was arranged for the day after her marriage to Rafael Sanchez-Lopez, a playwright. He appears in the full frame of some of the photographs but has been subsequently cropped out of the finished prints. Paloma Picasso is known today for her cosmetics, her perfume empire and her modernist jewellery designs. In 1985 Horst photographed the couple's New York apartment for American *Vogue* in a twelve-page feature, highlighting Picasso's collection of her father's paintings and bronzes, and another of nineteenth-century serpentine vases and black Art Deco chairs by Emile-Jacques Ruhlmann.
Taken: New York, 1979

Published: French *Vogue*, December 1979 – January 1980, pp.328-9

Plate 118, DIANA VREELAND (1901-89)

Diana Dalziel was a true cosmopolitan, both by birth (she was Scottish, born and brought up in Paris) and by social interaction (she and her husband, T. Reed Vreeland, spent their time between London, Lausanne and New York). In 1937 she became Fashion Editor of *Harper's Bazaar* and is chiefly remembered for her sly and witty column 'Why Don't You ...' poking fun at the peccadilloes of the fashionable in the Depression years. In 1961 she was appointed Editor-in-Chief of *Vogue*, where, as a true original, she was able to give full rein to her tastes in fashion and for pithy aphorisms, 'Pink is the Navy Blue of India', and more complex ones: 'I loathe red with any orange in it – although curiously enough I loathe orange without red in it. When I say orange, I don't mean yellow-orange, I mean the red-orange of Bakst and Diaghilev, the orange that changed the century!' She told Lawford, 'One of the things I most wanted to do when I joined *Vogue* was to produce articles about people in their houses and gardens, where they felt at their best and most natural. I thought that Horst would be the ideal photographer for this.' Many of the subjects were Vreeland's friends: the de Rothschilds, Pucci, the Duke and Duchess of Windsor. Others were selected by word of mouth: Cy Twombly in Rome, Lord Eliot in Cornwall, the Queen Mother of Romania in Florence. Many of them ended up in *Vogue's Book of Houses, Gardens and People*. In twelve years, no one refused Vreeland and Horst. In the 1970s, sacked from *Vogue*, Vreeland embarked on another career as consultant to the Costume Institute of The Metropolitan Museum of Art, New York.
Taken: New York, 1979

Plate 119, TRUMAN CAPOTE (1924-84)

By the time Horst took this portrait, Capote's best years as a writer were behind him and he was, to some extent, an outcast from the Manhattan society he fought so assiduously to join. The previous year *Esquire* magazine published two excerpts from an uncompleted novel, posthumously published as *Answered Prayers*, which ridiculed many of the socialites who had befriended him. The extracts revealed that Capote's writing had lost the sparkle that had made *Breakfast at Tiffany's* (1961) or *The Grass Harp* (1951) so beguiling. Capote was born in New Orleans, the son of a sales agent-turned-clerk and a teenage Beauty Queen. He started writing fiction at the tender age of eight, and joined the *New Yorker* after leaving college. In 1948 his first novel, *Other Voices, Other Rooms*, was published. Other novels followed including *Breakfast at Tiffany's*, which established Holly Golightly as a heroine of contemporary American fiction and was made into a successful film. His lifelong interest in journalism led to his development of the 'non-fiction novel' and he produced the classic work *In Cold Blood*, filmed in 1967, about the murder of a wealthy Midwestern family by two drifters. Apart from this portrait, Horst photographed Capote for an earlier interiors feature with the

latter's impish charm in evidence. On that occasion, Capote carefully placed centre-stage a copy of *Observations*, the book he produced with the star photographer of *Harper's Bazaar*, Richard Avedon, knowing of course that Horst's pictures were destined for its long-standing and frequently bitter rival magazine.
Taken: 1973

Plate 120, GILBERT AND GEORGE (GILBERT PROESCH b.1943, GEORGE PASSMORE b.1942)

Taken at face value, the colourful, conceptual art of Gilbert and George exists only to shock. Their interest in defining notions of male sexuality, especially in its working-class teenage manifestation, and predilection for 'taboo' subjects, perhaps exists to desensitize the public to the extent that it can no longer be shocked and might grow to accept, perhaps even admire, what formerly it had abhorred. Since leaving art college, Gilbert and George have made their lives into art as self-designated 'living sculptures'. Famously they stood in art galleries painted gold and singing *Underneath the Arches*, an English music hall turn, over and over again. Always on show, immaculate in tailored suits, they appear on the streets of London clad as quintessential English bachelors but with the inseparability and habitualness of old ladies at a seaside town. As 'living sculptures' they seem to welcome photographers at all times and a book devoted to representations of themselves from 1968 to 1997 showcases portraits by Cecil Beaton, David Bailey, Wolfgang Tillmans among dozens of others. Few of the photographers, if any at all, have revealed anything about the artists that they did not want known. They are brilliant deflators of art world bombast, its manipulators *non pareil*. In interviews they speak as one and as richly ironical: 'We don't enjoy life, no. We already gave our life away for our art. We're the dead rabbit on the plate. We want to spill our blood, our brains, our seed for art.'
Taken: Horst's house, Oyster Bay, 1970s

Plate 121, ROY LICHTENSTEIN (1923-97)

Before becoming successful as an artist, Lichtenstein, born in New York City in 1923, worked in Cleveland as an engineering draughtsman and graphic designer, and later as a teacher at Rutgers University. He was swayed enough by contemporary American consumer culture to give up the quasi-abstract expressionist style that characterizes his early work. Instead he looked to comic book images and other popular graphics. In 1961 he produced the large-scale comic-strip images with which he has become indelibly linked, reproducing meticulously by hand the lettering and 'Ben Day' dots typical of the screen process of printing comic books. This heralded his position in the vanguard of the 'Pop Art' movement and he was able to give up teaching in 1963. He consolidated his reputation with a series of black-and-white close-ups of domestic articles taken from found illustrations in newspapers and magazines. In 1969 he was given a large retrospective at the Guggenheim Museum in New York. In the 1980s he executed a mural (several storeys high) for the Equitable Life Assurance building in New York. The finished and published print of Horst's portrait of the artist in his Long Island studio did not include the fire extinguishers, iconic-looking in the context of Lichtenstein's work.
Taken: East Hampton, 1978, in his studio

Plate 122, CALVIN KLEIN (b.1942)

Calvin Klein started his own business in 1968, having spent the preceding five years designing for coat and suit manufacturers in New York City. He famously wheeled his earliest collection of suits and dresses on a dress-rail through Manhattan to the buyers of department stores: 'I was terrified a messenger would wrinkle the clothes' he told *Vogue*. In the early 1970s he branched out into designing less structured items, such as sportswear, slacks and sweaters. This heralded his mastery of minimalism and a clean understated look. He was prescient enough to see a niche for branded denim jeans and thereby launched the 'designer label' as a status symbol. He was among the first American designers to be aware of the power of marketing strategies. Campaigns for Calvin Klein gave him unprecedented coverage; whether it was Brooke Shields declaring that 'Nothing comes between me and my Calvins' or the giant billboards in Times Square for men's underwear (described by *Vogue* as his 'personal memo-pad to the universe'). In the mid-1990s he sold his underwear company for a staggering $64 million. The *New York Times* called him simply 'a phenomenon of our times'.
Taken: New York, 1984, for *GQ* magazine

Plate 123, PRINCESS STEPHANIE OF MONACO (b.1965)

The epitome of a modern European princess – beautiful, headstrong, rebellious and strong-willed – Princess Stephanie has seldom been far from the headlines and the lens of the paparazzi since 13 September 1982 when, at the age of seventeen, she was involved in a car crash that left her mother Princess Grace fatally injured. From then on, her life appears to have been increasingly fractured and she has picked up the threads of several promising careers only to drop them again: photographer, businesswoman, dress designer (she worked with Marc Bohan at Dior) and fashion model. Horst photographed her in this role for a skin-care advertisement. She has also launched her own perfume line and opened a café. In France she has had success as a recording artist, releasing three albums including *Live Your Life* (1986) and the eponymously titled *Stephanie* (1991). She has also featured in a duet with Michael Jackson. Her private life has been equally turbulent with high-profile relationships, including one with her personal bodyguard.
Taken: 'La Prairie' campaign, New York, 1985

Plate 124, ISABELLA ROSSELLINI (b.1952)

The daughter of Roberto Rossellini and Ingrid Bergman, it was almost inevitable that she would become an actress but she resisted it for some time. She has been a translator of Italian, a teacher, and the New York correspondent for an Italian television channel. As an actress she appeared with Mikhail Baryshnikov in *White Nights* (1985) and the following year she was cast by David Lynch in his controversial *Blue Velvet*. Of her role in the film, she famously remarked: 'David Lynch came out

of it a genius. I came out of it a fat girl'. She has also appeared in *Wild at Heart* (1990) and *The Funeral* and *Big Night* (both 1996). As well as being one of *People* magazine's 'Fifty Most Beautiful People in the World' for two years running (1990 and 1991), she was also a fixture in the advertising pages of glossy magazines as the face of cosmetics company Lancôme. The company signed her up for eight years. She now develops her own cosmetics line with Lancaster. Horst photographed her mother several times – 'she had a radiance' – and here captures the daughter's radiance, exclusively under contract to Lancôme, as part of an advertising campaign for its 'Black Lace'.
Taken: 'Black Lace' campaign, for Lancôme, 1984

Plate 125, RAOUL JULIA (1940-94)

The Puerto Rican-born actor achieved worldwide recognition for his role as Gomez in two live-action films based on Charles Addams' *Addams Family* cartoons. But the success of that lightweight role overshadowed a versatile and brilliant stage career on Broadway and beyond. He received three Tony nominations, most famously for his sinister performance as MacHeath in Brecht's *Threepenny Opera*. He was also a fixture in the classics from the *The Cherry Orchard* to *King Lear*, *The Taming of the Shrew* (with Meryl Streep) and *Othello* (to Richard Dreyfus's Iago). He also appeared in Peter Hall's Broadway production of Pinter's *Betrayal*. On screen he was memorable alongside Faye Dunaway in *The Eyes of Laura Mars* (1978) and as William Hurt's cellmate in *Kiss of the Spider Woman* (1985). He appeared predictably enough in many films with a Latin American theme, not least *Havana* (1990), *Tequila Sunrise* (1988) and the lead role in *Romero* (1989) about the assassination of the Salvadorean archbishop and his last film, *Chico*, about the life of Chico Mendes.
Taken: New York, 1982, for *Esquire* magazine

Plate 126, DEBBIE HARRY (b.1954)

Of all the American bands to come out of the 'New Wave' movement of the mid- to late 1970s, Blondie were by far the most commercially successful. Not least for the allure of their platinum-blonde front person, Debbie Harry, which gave them a slight edge over the likes of The Ramones and Talking Heads. A little older than most of these contemporaries (she was thirty-two when Blondie had its first hit record), Debbie Harry had started out as a waitress at the New York rock venue Max's Kansas City and later became a fixture at the notorious C.B.G.B club. Harry's movie-starlet looks and catchy songs (the Shangri-las meet the Beach Boys), dubbed 'Power Pop' by music journalists, had great commercial appeal. Their first three albums were worldwide best sellers. Each track of their fourth, *Eat to the Beat* (1979), was accompanied by a promotional video, the first time this had been done and a precursor to the proliferation of the video as a marketing weapon. By the early 1980s, Blondie fragmented with each band member pursuing other projects. Harry released a solo album, *Koo Koo* (1981). Still contractually obliged to produce a last album, the band members re-formed and it is from this period that Horst's portrait dates.
Taken: 1988

Plate 127, ERTÉ (1892-1990)

One of the last century's most exotic characters, who also happened to be one of its most innovative set and costume designers (famously for Diaghilev), was Romain de Tirtoff, better known by the French pronunciation of his intitals 'RT' – Erté. The writer Patrick Kinmonth quotes a contemporary account of his explosive début, 'In that brilliant audience all eyes were fixed on one of the boxes where two of Paul Poiret's models were sitting, accompanied by four gentlemen in impeccable evening dress. One model was an attractive blond but the other, with her scarlet turban, was irresistible, wearing her remarkable ensemble with an air and a sense of style that few models are lucky enough to possess....' Erté's was a rarefied world wherein to rehearse for a month the entrance to a fancy dress ball with the master of the Opera was not considered unusual. Born in 1892 in St Petersburg, he was still working at the age of eighty-eight, designing the sets for a production of *Der Rosenkavalier* at Glyndebourne. He was present at some of the legendary artistic events: the first night of Nijinsky's scandalous *L'Aprés-Midi d'un Faune*, the first performance of Stravinsky's *The Rite of Spring*, the début of Prokofiev and many performances by the great Pavlova.
Taken: Barbados, 1986

Plate 128, BRUCE WEBER (b.1946)

Bruce Weber made his name in fashion photography in the 1980s by creating fictitious worlds of sunny privilege for Ralph Lauren adverts and youthful, erotically charged ones for the Calvin Klein campaigns. Thus, he almost single-handedly shifted the emphasis from the clothes to those wearing them; the 'fashion' in 'fashion photography' never looked so oblique. His brilliant and inventive photographs for British *Vogue* betray a wide-ranging knowledge of photographic history where traces of August Sander or Edward Weston, say, are clearly in evidence and always acknowledged. His wide points of reference pay homage to Willa Cather, Italian neo-Realist cinema, Chet Baker and Georgia O'Keeffe. In the end, though, as the writer Martin Harrison has put it: '... with implacable determination he was consistently pushing the fashion photograph into becoming a Bruce Weber photograph'. Weber has redefined the depiction of male sexuality with a strong emphasis on physical beauty fused with a romantic, crepuscular sensuality. His books of photographs are prized by collectors and he has an equally uncompromising concomitant career as a film-maker. The ideals of classical sculpture frequently pervade his work, giving his male figures a heroic aura, an influence he shares with Horst and Huene. Weber is seldom photographed without his dogs (at least one of his books is devoted to them) and never, since his days as a model, without his beard or trademark bandana.
Taken: New York, 1988

Plate 129, KERRY HARPER

'Right from the start', Horst told writer Nancy Hall-Duncan, 'the editors in Paris let me create my own fantasies.' The world Horst conjured up rarely changed, apart from a brief and mostly unsuccessful attempt at the American *plein-air* naturalism

favoured by mid-century *Vogue*. His settings were always highly stylized and preferably in studio. His manipulation of studio lights elevated his sitters to goddesses of beauty and glamour. His monumentally carved sets made unreal worlds with frequent references to classical antiquity. This artificiality found many admirers, some overt like Robert Mapplethorpe, who acknowledged his influence in his portraits, nudes and flowers, and some not so open such as Cecil Beaton. Horst only ever used studio floods, as he thought strobes 'show everything too clearly'. In the opinion of one commentator, 'Common studio props, when subjected to Horst's masterful illumination and composition, become something of greater significance than their lowly reality of cardboard panels and plaster props.'
Taken: New York, 1980

Plate 130, KARL LAGERFELD (b.1938)
From a wealthy German and Swedish background, Lagerfeld was sent to Paris to finish his studies and by the age of sixteen he was working with the couturier Pierre Balmain. He left after three years to work for Jean Patou and then to freelance for various fashion houses including Krizia and Chloë and the shoe designer Charles Jourdan. In the mid-1960s he began to design furs for the Fendi sisters of Rome. However, he is best known for the collections that bear his own name and for steering the house of Chanel into the modern age. His reinterpretations of signatures from the legacy of Coco Chanel, most notably with the Chanel suit and the monogrammed double 'C', are witty, ironical and commercially successful. With his trademark pigtail and signature fan, he resembles a courtly eighteenth-century aesthete, and his wide-ranging interests which go far beyond the cutting of cloth, have secured his reputation as one of the fashion world's intellectual designers. A great admirer of Horst's purity of vision, he told British television that 'some photographers become famous with fashion and then they were too good for fashion. Most of them will never be remembered for what they did after or instead, but Horst never gave the impression that he was beyond fashion.'
Taken: 1980

Plate 131, JERRY HALL (b.1956)
Texan-born Jerry Hall has been a successful model since the 1970s and more recently an occasional actress. Outside the pages of *Vogue*, where she was a favourite of the photographers Norman Parkinson and Terence Donovan and the illustrator Antonio, she received wider coverage as the cover girl of Roxy Music's album *Siren* and featured in the video accompanying Bryan Ferry's single *Let's Stick Together*. After a romance with Ferry, she left him for his friend Mick Jagger in the 1980s and they married in 1990. Hall and Jagger's relationship was a tempestuous one and in 1999 Jerry Hall filed for divorce. Along with her friend Iman, Jerry Hall is one of the few well-known faces of the 1970s to continue, when either chooses, to work as a model today. She has also had a modest career as an actress with parts in films such as *Batman* (as girlfriend of Jack Nicholson's 'Joker') and on stage in *Bus Stop* and more recently as Mrs Robinson in

The Graduate. This photograph of her comes from a fashion shoot for French *Vogue* taken by Horst in Barbados. Mick Jagger and their children Elizabeth and James also appear in the 12-page story, as does Horst's manager, Rick Tardiff.
Taken: In a Gianni Versace jump suit, Barbados, 1986
Published: In French *Vogue*, May 1986, p.246

Plate 132, DURAN DURAN
Formed in Birmingham in 1978, the pop band, whose core members were Simon Le Bon, Nick Rhodes, Andy Taylor and Roger Taylor, took their name from a character in Roger Vadim's film *Barbarella* and aimed to become 'Chic crossed with the Sex Pistols'. With Spandau Ballet and others, they spearheaded the 'New Romantic' movement and released their first singles, *Planet Earth* and *My Own Way*, in 1987. In the early days of MTV, the band were pioneers in realizing the potential of the promotional video and their record company appeared to have limitless funds to court the new medium. They enlisted directors such as Godley and Creme and Russell Mulcahy to create ever more lavish scenarios for their singles in ever more exotic places. It helped that Le Bon had once been a child actor and knew how to perform in front of lights and cameras. The video for *Girls on Film* created controversy and publicity when banned by both MTV and British television. Various pressures, not least constant touring, led to the band's break-up in the 1990s, but several members re-formed it later to great success again. Horst was asked to photograph them as a try-out for an album cover in 1986. On the same trip to England he photographed Le Bon's wife, the model Yasmin, for a *Vogue* fashion shoot. He was slightly baffled by the band, their world so far removed from his, but was pleased that they wanted to know 'all about Madame so-and-so and all the people from the thirties'.
Taken: London, 1986

Plate 133, CATHERINE BAILEY
The writer Fay Weldon has described Catherine Bailey (née Dyer) as the personification of 'the abstract notion of Beauty'. Apart from being a highly regarded model, she is the wife of the photographer David Bailey, a *Vogue* contributor for nearly forty years until recently. Bailey had taken a penetrating portrait of Horst to accompany an article in the magazine, celebrating not only Horst's professional longevity, but also the 150th anniversary of the birth of photography. Although Valentine Lawford wrote in 1984 that Horst always 'felt out of his element in England, a feeling that persists to this day', at the age of eighty-three he accepted an invitation to a symposium, 'Makers of Photographic History', hosted by Britain's National Museum of Photography at Bradford. He also held a workshop with *Vogue* Fashion Editor Lucinda Chambers, photographing Catherine Bailey in clothes from the British collections. The results are a homage to his distinguished past. He reminded his audience at Bradford that 'there is always real elegance somewhere', and admonished them to seek it out.
Taken: Bradford, England, 1989

ACKNOWLEDGEMENTS

In the preparation of this exhibition I have been greatly helped and encouraged by a considerable number of people on both sides of the Atlantic. In New York, the ever-enthusiastic Charles D. Scheips, Ena Wojciechowski and Anthony Petrillose at the Condé Nast Archive. Charles gave generously of his time in introducing me to his fellow staff, and the highly organised and well-run back issues and archive print collections, expertly indexed and digitized. Elsewhere in the city I was encouraged by Carmen Dell'Orefice, Kathryn Abbe, Frances McLaughlin-Gill, Anne Horton, Jill Quasha, James Watters, Etheleen Staley and Taki Wise, who all shared my enthusiasm for the project. At the Horst house in Oyster Bay, Hans Mayr and Jennifer Gyr provided generous hospitality and invaluable assistance.

Back in London further help was given by Rosalind Crowe, Philippe Garner, Russell Harris, Paul Lyon-Maris, Philip Hoare and Hugo Vickers. Lisa Hodgkin in charge of the British *Vogue* Library showed immense patience while I spent days trying to search though sixty years of three editions of *Vogue* for lost references. At the National Portrait Gallery I am very grateful to my many colleagues who gave help and assistance, including Emma Marlow, Hazel Sutherland and the PR and Development Department, Claire Everitt, Clare Freestone, Jude Simmons, and particularly Beatrice Hosegood, who kept control of loans and administration. Anjali Bulley and the Publications Department provided much creative editorial help. Thanks also to Price Watkins for the elegant design of the catalogue.

I should also like to thank Robin Muir for his huge contribution to the catalogue in writing, at very short notice and with unfailing good humour, extremely comprehensive notes on the plates. Finally, I must thank Andrew Cowan and Tim Jefferies of Hamiltons, who for over twenty years have helped promote excellence in photographic exhibitions, for providing us with the unique opportunity of mounting this exhibition.

Terence Pepper
December 2000

PICTURE CREDITS